Routledge Revivals

Exchange Rate Efficiency and the Behavior of International Asset Markets

This book, first published in 1992, examines the subject of foreign exchange market efficiency and, in particular, the effectiveness of central bank intervention in the market. This book is ideal for students of economics.

AF833224

Exchange Rate Efficiency and the Behavior of International Asset Markets

Kathryn Mary Dominguez

Routledge
Taylor & Francis Group

First published in 1992
by Garland Publishing, Inc.

This edition first published in 2015 by Routledge
2 Park Square, Milton Park, Abingdon, Oxon, OX14 4RN
and by Routledge
711 Third Avenue, New York, NY 10017

Routledge is an imprint of the Taylor & Francis Group, an informa business

© 1992 Kathryn Mary Dominguez

The right of Kathryn Mary Dominguez to be identified as author of this work has been asserted by her in accordance with sections 77 and 78 of the Copyright, Designs and Patents Act 1988.

All rights reserved. No part of this book may be reprinted or reproduced or utilised in any form or by any electronic, mechanical, or other means, now known or hereafter invented, including photocopying and recording, or in any information storage or retrieval system, without permission in writing from the publishers.

Publisher's Note
The publisher has gone to great lengths to ensure the quality of this reprint but points out that some imperfections in the original copies may be apparent.

Disclaimer
The publisher has made every effort to trace copyright holders and welcomes correspondence from those they have been unable to contact.

A Library of Congress record exists under LC control number: 92027792

ISBN 13: 978-1-138-83876-5 (hbk)
ISBN 13: 978-1-315-73382-1 (ebk)
ISBN 13: 978-1-138-83878-9 (pbk)

Exchange Rate Efficiency and the Behavior of International Asset Markets

KATHRYN MARY DOMINGUEZ

GARLAND PUBLISHING, INC.
NEW YORK & LONDON
1992

Copyright © 1992 by Kathryn Mary Dominguez
All rights reserved

Library of Congress Cataloging-in-Publication Data

Dominguez, Kathryn Mary.
Exchange rate efficiency and the behavior of international asset markets / Kathryn Mary Dominguez.
p. cm. — (The financial sector of the American economy)
Includes bibliographical references and index.
ISBN 0-8153-0961-9
1. Foreign exchange market. 2. Foreign exchange rates.
I. Title. II. Series.
HG3821.D68 1992
332.4'56—dc20 92-27792
CIP

Printed on acid-free, 250-year-life paper
Manufactured in the United States of America

To James

CONTENTS

CHAPTER 2
THE INFORMATIONAL ROLE OF OFFICIAL FOREIGN EXCHANGE INTERVENTION POLICY: THE SIGNALLING HYPOTHESIS

CHAPTER 3
THE PRICING OF FOREIGN EXCHANGE RISK IN THE STOCK MARKET: A TEST FOR INTERNATIONAL ECONOMIC INTERDEPENDENCE

PREFACE

This study was first submitted as a doctoral dissertation at Yale University in the spring of 1987. The subject of foreign exchange market efficiency, and, in particular, the effectiveness of central bank intervention in the market, has become extremely popular among academic researchers since that time. This renascent interest in exchange rate policy is at least in part due to its popularity in policy circles. The G-5 countries engaged in an unprecedented number of coordinated intervention operations in the late 1980s. Since other scholars and I have studied these later episodes in subsequent research, I have made no attempt to extend the empirical work in this inquiry beyond the original sample periods.

A drastically condensed version of Chapter 1 of this study was published in 1986 in *Economics Letters*. The Money Market Services, Inc. survey data on exchange rate expectations used in the study have subsequently been examined in numerous studies, most notably Dominguez and Frankel (1992a,b), Frankel and Froot (1987, 1990a,b), and Froot and Frankel (1989). Analysis of exchange rate expectations in the late 1980s largely confirm the results that were found for the early 1980s; the hypothesis of rational expectations is decisively rejected. In a related study, Ito (1990) finds evidence of heterogenous irrationality in a panel series of survey data compiled by the JCIF in Tokyo.

The signalling hypothesis, the subject of Chapter 2 of the thesis, has recently gained a modicum of acceptance among academics. Although many economists remain puzzled about how, when, and why intervention policy is effective, the signalling hypothesis is now viewed as a potential explanation. In a series of papers I have further tested the signalling hypothesis using U.S. and German intervention data in the 1980s. In a study published in 1990 in the *Carnegie-Rochester Series on Public Policy* I examine the five major episodes of coordinated G-5 intervention in the three year period 1985-1987. This time period is also examined by Obstfeld (1990). In Dominguez (1990b) and Dominguez and Frankel (1992a,b) we develop an econometric methodology that allows us to disentangle the portfolio and signalling effects of intervention on exchange rates. Our results suggest that it is the latter channel that is economically meaningful, although intervention operations are found to have a statistically significant effect on exchange rates through both channels.

The literature on exchange rate risk has expanded exponentially since I worked in the area as a graduate student. A number of empirical studies have convincingly documented that stock market returns are, to some extent, predictable using interest rates and dividend yields. The evidence presented in Chapter 3 using exchange rates remains controversial because the study only covers a five year period. Although the existence of an exchange rate risk premia is widely accepted, empirical tests that cover longer time horizons have been inconclusive.

ACKNOWLEDGMENTS

This dissertation would not have been possible without the support of many people. The encouragement, oversight, advice and comment of my dissertation committee members, Ray C. Fair and Matthew D. Shapiro, have been invaluable.

I am grateful to Yale University and the American Economics Association for tuition and fellowship support that allowed me to worry about financial research rather than my own finances.

The first chapter of the dissertation was written while I was an intern at the International Finance Division of the Federal Reserve Board in 1985-1986. I thank Neil Ericsson, Hali Edison, and Michael Gavin for their interest and support of this research. I am also grateful to seminar participants at the Federal Reserve Board for comments and criticisms.

The second chapter would not have been possible without the support of the Federal Reserve Board and the German Bundesbank. Both central banks provided me confidential data on their daily intervention operations for use in the empirical tests. I wish to thank, in particular, Dr. Ted Truman, Director of the International Division at the Fed and Dr. Franz Scholl, Director of the Bundesbank for their assistance in gaining access to the intervention data.

In addition, I have received many helpful comments and suggestions from Willem Buiter, Koichi Hamada, Stephen Ross, Robert Shiller and Roger Ibbotson. I also thank seminar participants at Yale, Princeton University, the Kennedy School at Harvard University, the Johns Hopkins University, the University of Rochester, UCLA, and Stanford University for discussion. Their criticisms greatly improved the quality of the analysis.

Finally, I owe a debt of gratitude to my parents for their unrelenting encouragement and support.

INTRODUCTION

I. THE ERA OF FLOATING EXCHANGE RATES

Since the breakdown of the Bretton Woods system of fixed exchange rates in 1973, a fundamental question for economic research has been the efficiency of the new floating exchange rate regime. Most mainstream economists had actively advocated the abandonment of fixed rates. Under the old system, relative currency prices were pegged to the dollar (and adjusted infrequently) on the basis of a modified gold standard. This system left currency values open to political manipulation and speculative attack as individuals anticipated central bank decisions to devalue currencies.

The theory of open economies suggested that many benefits would flow from the new floating exchange rate regime. Under floating rates, the relative price of countries' currencies would accurately reflect the relative underlying value of their economies. Currency values would adjust so as to reflect changes in international trade flows and the relative prices of traded goods, as caused by changes in the domestic structure of individual countries' economies. Relative currency prices would thereby equilibrate trade and capital flows between countries. Unlike the fixed rate regime, therefore, floating rates would prevent severe and sustained imbalances in countries' current accounts.

From the viewpoint of macroeconomic stabilization policy, floating rates were also expected to cause fundamental changes. They were expected to render fiscal policies less relevant; exchange rates would adjust to offset changes in spending that were not monetized. The power of monetary policies, in contrast, would be enhanced. Indeed a particular benefit of floating rates was the freedom they created for countries to pursue separate domestic monetary policies.

Since the advent of floating rates in 1973, however, there has been widespread disagreement about its economic effects. Exchange rate determination has not fit the standard predictions of floating-rate models. This is in part because the float has not been "clean," but rather managed by (sometimes coordinated) efforts on the part of the central banks of the developed countries. However, even apart from government intervention, the short-term behavior of rates has proven disquieting and difficult to analyze. Exchange rates have been found to be too volatile to be consistent with standard models of exchange rate determination (Huang (1981)), and prone to prolonged deviations from purchasing power parity (Frenkel (1981)).

Nor has the effect of floating rates on domestic macroeconomic policy been exactly as predicted by theory. During the early 1980s, the U.S. maintained the biggest expansionary fiscal policy in history; it was not quickly offset by simple exchange rate adjustments. Current account imbalances persisted far longer than theory can explain. Government attempts to "manage" the exchange rate have continued, despite an increasing rhetorical commitment to free trade. Yet there is no agreement on either the benefits of such intervention, or indeed its effectiveness in determining the direction of exchange rate movements.

Thus the era of floating exchange rates has raised many new theoretical and empirical questions for international finance and open economy macroeconomics. Neither the behavior of exchange rates themselves, nor the implications of their behavior, are yet well understood. This in turn poses a fundamental problem for domestic economic policy in an increasingly open world economic environment.

II. THE SCOPE OF THE THESIS

The thesis, which consists of three essays, attempts to provide new empirical evidence that is relevant to assessing three questions about the behavior and consequences of floating exchange rates. The first essay examines the expectational efficiency of four bilateral exchange rates, using new data that allow model-free efficiency tests. The second essay examines a central policy question in the floating exchange rate era: can sterilized intervention influence exchange rate movements? The third essay examines the effect of floating exchange rates on U.S. domestic asset markets, asking whether there is a measurable exchange rate risk premium associated with domestic asset pricing.

In the first essay, I examine whether exchange rates are rational in the sense dictated by the asset approach to exchange rate determination. This approach views bilateral exchange rates as aggregators of all relevant information about the current and future performance of two economies (Mussa (1976)). Exchange rates are viewed in a similar light as stock prices, as forward-looking measures of relative economic performance. This paradigm suggests that exchange rate movements should not be well explained by structural models that describe changes in current economic conditions. Rather, rate movements are caused by expectational surprises about the relative performance of the two economies in question (which may, of course, be unobservable). There is evidence to sustain the asset approach's central conjecture that rates are forward-looking, and react to new information that constitutes a surprise about future economic conditions. For example, it has been demonstrated that exchange rates react to the Federal Reserve Board's weekly money supply announcement, and inferentially, to changes in expectations about future monetary policy (Engel and Frankel (1984), Hardouvelis (1984)).

The asset approach derives much of its appeal from the fact that it contains direct, testable implications for exchange rate efficiency. In an informationally efficient market, asset prices must be unpredictable. If asset prices are predictable, then the market is consistently failing to incorporate information about future conditions in forming its predictions. The asset approach is supported by empirical evidence showing that a random walk model of exchange rates outperforms most standard, one-equation structural models of exchange rate determination (Meese and Rogoff (1983,1985)).

Nevertheless, the efficiency of exchange rate behavior, in the sense suggested by the asset approach, has proven quite difficult to test conclusively. The problem is that there is not a well-accepted risk/return relationship that describes exchange rate behavior. Given this, much of the recent evidence on asset market efficiency has been difficult to interpret. In particular, there is a large literature showing that the forward exchange rate is a biased predictor of future spot rates (Hansen and Hodrick (1980,1983), Cumby and Obstfeld (1981,1984)). This means either that exchange rates are inefficient, in the sense of the asset market approach, or that there is an (unspecified) risk premium influencing exchange rate movements.

The first chapter of the thesis circumvents this observability problem by testing the rationality, or efficiency in the asset market sense, of a series of direct observations of foreign exchange rate expectations. The expectations series is derived from a survey of professional foreign exchange forecasters, taken by a private survey organization that sells its survey results to other market participants. Other survey data supplied by the organization, in particular on money supply expectations, have been widely used by empiricists and found to be of high quality. Indeed empirical examinations of the money supply data conclude that it is rational (Grossman (1981), Urich and Wachtel (1981)). However, as yet no one has examined the properties of the (more recent) survey on exchange rate expectations.

The use of survey data makes it possible to test the central efficiency hypothesis of the asset approach--that expectations of future rates are unbiased with respect to actual, realized outcomes. By observing expectations directly, the problem of the risk premium embodied in observed forward and spot rates is avoided. The tests contained in Chapter 1 provide new evidence against the simple efficiency theory. Consensus expectations do not appear unbiased with respect to outcomes. Rather, expectations consistently lag realizations, and do not fully incorporate information available from forward rates. These results may be taken as evidence against the view that exchange markets operate efficiently. However, the evidence may also be viewed within the context of a Bayesian or bubble process model of expectations. Either way, the results complement other recent evidence in rejecting the simple form of the RE hypothesis.

The second essay focusses on the effects of central bank intervention in foreign exchange markets, examining, in particular, sterilized intervention. The floating exchange rate regime has been characterized by at times heavy intervention by central banks, including the U.S. Federal Reserve Board. From a theoretical viewpoint, it has not been clear what legitimate economic purpose intervention serves, in a system in which currency values are supposed to reflect economic values and equilibrate trade patterns. Nor, from an empirical viewpoint, has it been clear whether these interventions actually affect exchange rates, despite the often vivid association between the central bank's stated policy goals, and the ultimate behavior of the currency in question (such as, for example, the apparently "engineered" slide of the dollar in the fall of 1985).

These concerns apply particularly to sterilized intervention, because the construction of this policy seems to guarantee its ineffectiveness in changing currency values. 'Sterilized intervention' describes the action of a central bank in purchasing or selling foreign exchange reserves in combination with an open-market operation that leaves the monetary base unchanged. The net result of a sterilized intervention is a change in the relative supply outstanding of foreign and dollar-denominated assets, and no change in the monetary base.

In Chapter 2 of the thesis, I offer a theory and a series of empirical tests of the effects of daily sterilized intervention on spot exchange rates. The theory revives Milton Friedman's 1953 observation about the potential role played by sterilized intervention, suggesting that it can function as a signal of future central bank monetary policy. This hypothesis is discussed and formalized within the context of modern signalling theory. I argue that sterilized intervention is an ideal signal, as it entails no deviation by the central bank from its chosen monetary policy course. If intervention indeed serves as a leading indicator of monetary policy, conveying information to the market, it is shown that it could have significant effects on exchange rate formation.

I am able to test the signalling theory due to a unique opportunity to work with the daily data on sterilized intervention by the Federal Reserve Board and the German Bundesbank, covering the period 1977-1985. These data were obtained under confidentiality agreements with both central banks. The results of the tests presented in Chapter 2 are consistent with the notion that the Fed uses intervention to signal future monetary policy. However, results also show that in other periods, the Fed may also have tried to use intervention to target the dollar in a manner inconsistent with monetary policy.

Chapter 3 of the thesis presents a series of tests of whether foreign exchange risk is priced in domestic asset markets, in the sense of Ross's (1976) Arbitrage Pricing Theory. These tests provide new evidence about the relationship between domestic and international capital markets. In particular, the tests provide important evidence about the factors governing asset price determination in the U.S., asking specifically whether international as well as domestic factors are fundamental to the behavior of asset prices. The tests can be interpreted as showing that changes in the relative performance of foreign economies, as reflected by changes in the exchange rate, affect the risk/return equilibrium in domestic asset markets.

The tests follow the approach of other recent tests of the APT, which have attempted to identify observable factors that are responsible for systematic risk across all domestic U.S. assets. Several authors have shown that innovations in important macroeconomic factors, such as industrial production, inflation, and the difference between low-grade corporate and long-term government bonds dominate the effect of the market portfolio in explaining cross-sectional risk/return relationships (Chan, Chen, and Hsieh (1985), Chen, Roll and Ross (1986)). These tests both validate the basic tenets of the APT theory, and shed important light on the relationship between macroeconomic activity and asset pricing in the economy.

In Chapter 3, I use daily data for all firms on the C.R.S.P. stock returns tape for the period 1980-1985, daily changes in the dollar/deutschemark exchange rate, and daily changes in the three-month Treasury Bill rate to test for the existence of a foreign exchange risk premium on U.S. corporate securities. The tests use the Fama and MacBeth (1973) technique for testing for a cross-sectional, ex-ante risk/return relationship. Portfolios of securities are formed on the basis of industry classifications; historical covariances with exchange rates, interest rates and the equal-weighted market index are then estimated. These covariances (betas) are then used in cross-sectional tests to examine whether higher covariance with each factor predicts higher ex-ante cross-sectional returns. The results show foreign exchange risk to be non-diversifiable across the domestic asset market; exchange rate risk is priced in the sense of the APT.

These results have implications for a number of important issues in finance. The tests first provide further confirmation for the APT, showing that international as well as domestic factors underlie the equilibrium returns structure observed in asset markets. These results are suggestive when viewed within the context of the ongoing debate over the internationalization of asset markets. They show that the relative performance of other countries' economies affect the risk/return relationship in American asset markets, and therefore, that the U.S. stock market is "open" in the sense of being affected by changes in the international economy.

Exchange Rate Efficiency and the Behavior of International Asset Markets

CHAPTER 1

Are Foreign Exchange Forecasts Rational? New Evidence From Survey Data

I. INTRODUCTION

For fifteen years, theories of expectations formation--particularly the rational expectations hypothesis--have been at the forefront of economic research. More recently empirical work has begun to focus on testing the operational validity of rational expectations.[1] Survey evidence on the formation of expectations has, as a result, become an important data source. This chapter examines the rationality of a newly available set of survey data on foreign exchange rate forecasts provided by Money Market Services (MMS).[2]

Section II of this chapter describes the joint hypothesis problem implicit in tests of market rationality and the consequential usefulness of direct observations of market expectations to circumvent the problem. Section III describes the rationality tests, the data and the method of estimation used in this study. Section IV presents the regression results of the rationality tests using consensus forecasts. Finally, Section V provides a summary and conclusions.

II. THE JOINT HYPOTHESIS PROBLEM AND A CIRCUMVENTION

A. Exchange Rate Efficiency

The collapse of the Bretton Woods fixed exchange rate system and subsequent change to market-determined exchange rates in 1973 dramatically changed the research focus of empirical work on exchange rates. The economic argument for changing to a floating exchange rate regime centered largely on the issue of market efficiency.[3] In an efficient market, exchange rates should fully reflect all available information, and rational economic decisions based on these relative prices should insure an efficient allocation of resources. After the change to flexible exchange rates, empirical research focused on testing the efficiency hypothesis, i.e., testing whether floating exchange rates did indeed serve as efficient aggregators of information.

One approach to testing the informational efficiency of exchange rates, advocated by Fama (1970), argues that efficiency requires that actual prices (or rates of return) follow a "fair game" process relative to expected equilibrium prices (or rates of return). In other words, in an efficient market investors should not be able to earn excess profit using publicly available information, where excess profit is defined relative to an expected equilibrium rate of return. In order to test the efficiency of foreign exchange markets, it is, therefore, necessary first to specify a model of the equilibrium risk/return relationship between currencies. The efficiency test is then a test of a joint hypothesis, that the equilibrium model specified is correct and that the market is efficient, preventing pure arbitrage opportunities between currencies or over time. The main problem confronting this approach lies in the first part of the joint hypothesis: specifying the equilibrium model. No clear specification of the expected return to holding foreign currency has emerged, and hence evidence on excess returns is difficult to interpret.

A second approach to testing foreign exchange market efficiency lies in the development of structural exchange rate models, which explain the path of exchange rates in terms of observable macroeconomic variables. While a number of models have been developed to describe the determination of flexible exchange rates, no one model has gained general acceptance by the profession.[4] Empirical tests of structural models in the literature have had some success in isolating the important explanatory variables.[5] However, Meese and Rogoff (1983,1985) find that neither structural (one-equation) models nor univariate time series techniques improve on a random walk model of exchange rates in spite of the fact that they base their forecasts on realized values of future explanatory variables. Fair (1986), in contrast, shows that, within the context of a large macroeconomic model, structural exchange rate equations forecast better out-of-sample than random walk or autoregressive models. The appropriate structure to use in modelling exchange rates, and thus determining exchange rate efficiency, remains unresolved.

B. Forward Market Efficiency

One path that researchers have taken to side-step the "lack of an equilibrium rate" problem is to examine the forward exchange rate, testing whether it is an unbiased predictor of future spot rates. Forward market studies can exploit Fama's "fair-game" approach by testing whether there exist unusual profit opportunities in the forward exchange market.

An investor can sign a forward contract at time t to purchase foreign currency at time t+k at a price, $f_{t,k} = s_t + (i_{t,k} - i^*_{t,k})$, where the variables are the logarithm of the k-period-ahead forward rate, $f_{t,k}$, the logarithm of the spot exchange rate, s_t, and the k-period-ahead interest rate, $i_{t,k}$; foreign variables are denoted with an asterisk (*). At time t+k the investor can turn around and sell the foreign currency at the spot price s_{t+k}. Presumably the "rational" investor will only enter into a forward contract if he or she expects that:[6]

$$E_t s_{t+k} \geq s_t + (i_{t,k} - i^*_{t,k}) = f_{t,k} \qquad (1)$$

where E_t is the expectation conditional on information available at time t. Further, if the forward market is efficient, then expected forward market profits should be zero; $E_t s_{t+k} - f_{t,k} = 0$. However, forward market efficiency does not preclude the existence of a risk premium, defined as the excess expected return demanded by investors for assuming the risk of future changes in exchange rates. So the relevant forward market equilibrium condition may include an additional term :

$$E_t s_{t+k} - risk_{t,k} - f_{t,k} = 0 \tag{2}$$

Forward market tests therefore involve the joint hypothesis of a specific risk/return relationship and rationality.

Empirical tests of formal models of exchange rate risk have had little success in characterizing the nature of the risk premium.[7] Consequently, recent work has generally tested for risk neutrality and rationality, consistently rejecting this joint hypothesis,[8] but it remains unclear whether this rejection shows expectations to be biased and inefficient, or whether it reflects the existence of a time-varying (and elusive) risk premium.

C. Survey Expectations

The benefits to be derived from studying exchange market expectations should be clear. Survey data allow single-hypothesis, model-free tests of rationality in foreign currency markets. Studies that reject the joint hypothesis of spot and forward market efficiency cannot distinguish whether it was the failure of the equilibrium model, or the failure of rational expectations, that led to the rejection. In order to test the rationality hypothesis directly, therefore, expectations data is essential.

Although many readers will not require justification for using survey data, such data have often been dismissed by economists claiming that surveys are not representative of the agents who drive the market. The usual example cited is that of a market with only a few rational agents, but whose actions ensure rationality at the margin despite the irrationality of the majority (Mishkin (1981)).

The rationality-on-the-margin argument may bear relevance. However, no one has been able to provide convincing theoretical evidence showing how such a marginal condition might apply. Indeed, newer work[9] concludes that only under a very restricted set of conditions is rationality of some but not all agents sufficient to ensure rationality in the market result overall.

There is little debate that use of massive surveys along the lines of the Livingston series[10] is likely to bias the tests of rationality improperly towards rejection (in the sense of examining the rationality of macroeconomically irrelevant expectations). One way around the problem is to use surveys of professional forecasters. Since the success and indeed livelihood of a professional forecaster is presumably a function of accuracy, the use of professional forecasters as representative agents will ensure that those examined are those most likely to have the most rational expectations. The performance of professional forecasters therefore may be taken to define an upper bound on the expectational accuracy of agents in the economy as a whole (Nordhaus and Durlauf (1984)).

The methodology and respondent sample for the Money Market Services survey inspire unusual confidence. The thirty respondents are professional exchange rate forecasters; most work in foreign currency trading divisions of major commercial banks. The standard arguments against surveys--in particular, that they do not adequately reflect the decisive players in the market--are clearly less problematic with this sample than in most surveys. There is equal reason to have confidence in the survey's design and execution. Unlike many surveys which are administered through the mail, the MMS survey is conducted by telephone each Wednesday afternoon eastern standard time (EST). Such accurate timing minimizes the problem of different information sets across forecasters.[11]

III. DESCRIPTION OF THE TESTS, THE DATA, AND ESTIMATION

A. Tests of the Rational Expectations Hypothesis

The rational expectations hypothesis states that rational participants in the market have expectations that are optimal forecasts using all available information. The usual rationality tests found in the literature have been of two basic sorts: the first tests whether the forecasts are unbiased estimates of the actual series, and the second, whether forecasts incorporate all available information. Commonly, unbiasedness is tested by running the OLS regression:

$$s_{t+k} = \alpha_0 + \alpha_1 E_t s_{t+k} + u_{t,k} \tag{3}$$

where s_{t+k} is the k-period ahead spot exchange rate, E_t is the expectation at time t and $u_{t,k}$ is the forecast error. ($E_t s_{t+k}$ has typically been proxied with the time t, k-period-ahead forward rate.) Unbiasedness requires the joint hypothesis that $\alpha_0=0$ and $\alpha_1=1$.

The second type of test checks that relevant information is included in the forecast. Clearly if any information available at time t is systematically excluded from the forecast and would improve the forecast, then the forecast is not optimal, and therefore also not rational. In order to test whether forecasts do incorporate relevant information we regress forecast errors on specific data[12] that were available to the forecasters. One piece of information that a rational forecaster should consider is his or her most recent forecast error. This can be tested by running the regression:

$$s_{t+k} - E_t s_{t+k} = \beta_0 + \beta_1 (s_t - E_{t-k} s_t) + \eta_{t,k} \tag{4}$$

If the forecast errors exhibit a significant non-zero mean and serial correlation[13] (significant β_1) then this implies that the information contained in past forecast errors was not fully utilized in forming future predictions.

When the information set is restricted to a constant and the current or lagged set of forecasts, the tests examine what is commonly called the weak version of rational expectations (RE). When other, publicly available regressors are included, the tests examine the semi-strong form of RE. Semi-strong rationality tests take the form:

$$s_{t+k} - E_t s_{t+k} = \delta_0 + \delta_1 z_t + \epsilon_{t,k} \tag{5}$$

where z_t is a variable that embodies available information relevant to the forecasts. The hypothesis of informational efficiency requires that the coefficient on z_t and the constant be insignificantly different than zero.

Results of these three rationality tests will be presented in the following section. The remainder of this section will describe the data and econometric technique used in the regression estimation.

B. Description of the Data

Money Market Services surveys bilateral (dollar) exchange rate forecasts of the British pound, the West German mark, the Swiss franc and the Japanese yen. From January 1983 to October 10, 1984 forecasters were asked every other week (bi-weekly) to predict spot rates two weeks and three months from the day of the survey. Since October 24, 1984 forecasters have been asked weekly for their one-week-ahead forecasts and bi-weekly for their one-month-ahead forecasts. Throughout its existence, the survey has typically been taken after 12 pm EST: the forecasters therefore have information on the noon New York spot rate and can calculate (but are not told) their forecast error from their two-week or one-week previous short-horizon forecast. If the forecast date falls on a holiday or weekend, the date is switched to the next business day. In contrast to the one- and two-week-ahead cases, forecasters will not be able to calculate their previous one- or three-month-ahead forecast error before the next survey.

Temporal alignment of exchange rate data is extremely important, as the rates can vary as much within a day as across days. The actual market spot and forward rates used in the regression analyses are taken from Data Resources Inc. and the New York Federal Reserve Bank International Balance of Payments Data Base. All series are in logarithms[14] and are the average of the New York certified noon bid and ask rates. Each MMS median[15] prediction was carefully aligned with the corresponding spot rate, and, in the one- and three-month-ahead cases, the one- and three-month-ahead forward rate. The relevant institutional features of forward contract delivery timing have been taken into account as discussed in detail by both Meese and Singleton (1982) and Hsieh (1984).[16]

C. The Estimation Method

In the following section, all models using one- and two-week-ahead forecasts were estimated over the four currencies using seemingly unrelated regressions (SUR). Currency arbitrage implies that error terms across currencies are likely to be contemporaneously correlated. Zellner's (1962) joint estimation technique resulted in an efficiency gain because individual equation disturbances were contemporaneously correlated.

While the one- and two-week-ahead forecasts are nonoverlapping, the one- and three-month-ahead forecasts are surveyed bi-weekly and therefore do overlap. If the sample size were not already small, constructing a nonoverlapping data set would be preferable. Hansen and Hodrick (1980,1983) and Hayashi and Sims (1983) discuss the econometric problem arising when the sampling interval is finer than the interval over which forecasts are made. In our case, because the actual spot rate corresponding to the preceding period one- and three-month-ahead forecast is not available to the survey respondents for another two or six periods respectively, the disturbances are no longer guaranteed to be serially uncorrelated. The OLS estimate of α_1 in a regression of the form $s_{t+k} = \alpha_0 + \alpha_1 E_t s_{t+k} + u_{t,k}$ should remain consistent as long as $u_{t,k}$ and $E_t s_{t+k}$ are not correlated, but the standard errors will be biased when any lagged values of $u_{t,k}$ are not in the information set (ie. $E[u_{t,k} | u_{t-j,k}]$ is non-zero for all $k>1$ and $j<k$, where k=forecast horizon and j=sampling interval).

Consider the case of MMS respondents who are asked, on a bi-weekly basis, for their month-ahead forecasts. At the time they respond to the survey, they will not know (with certainty) what their previous forecast error was, since only two weeks elapse between forecasts. Consequently, errors can persist over short periods, and $E[u_{t,4} | u_{t-2,4}]$ is non-zero. Hansen (1982) and Hansen and Hodrick (1983) present large sample properties of a class of generalized method of moments estimators that allow for both serially correlated and heteroskedastic disturbance terms.

Cumby and Obstfeld (1984) provide a formal test for conditional homoskedasticity: that the conditional covariances of forecast errors with respect to lagged forecasts are constants. Under the assumption that the survey forecasts are unbiased predictors of future spot rates, the expectation of the square of the forecast error from the unbiasedness regression:

$$s_{t+k} - s_t = a_0 + a_1(E_t s_{t+k} - s_t) + v_{t,k} \tag{6}$$

with respect to all instruments available at time t, z_t, should be constant:

$$E(\hat{v}_{t,k}^2 | z_t) = \sigma \tag{7}$$

This can be tested by estimating an equation of the form:

$$\hat{v}_{t,k}^2 = b_0 + b_1(E_t s_{t+k} - s_t) + b_2(E_t s_{t+k} - s_t)^2 + \zeta_{t,k} \tag{8}$$

and testing the hypothesis that $b_1 = b_2 = 0$. Table 1.1 provides results of the conditional homoskedasticity tests of one- and three-month-ahead survey forecast errors. The instrumental variables used were the time t expected depreciation ($E_t s_{t+k} - s_t$) and the same variable squared for the four countries. In two of the eight cases, the null hypothesis of conditional homoskedasticity is rejected.

Hsieh's (1984) results with non-overlapping data suggest that tests assuming conditional homoskedasticity when the assumption is not justified often underestimate the standard errors of the OLS coefficients, biasing toward rejection. All the one- and three-month-ahead equations in the following section are therefore estimated with Hansen's (1982) case(v) heteroskedasticity consistent covariance matrix; assuming a first-order moving average process for the bi-weekly one-month-ahead disturbances and a fifth-order moving average process for the bi-weekly three-month-ahead disturbances. The estimate of the covariance matrix is obtained by calculating a consistent estimate of the spectral density matrix at frequency zero of the vector stochastic process $[s_t'\hat{v}_t]$ (where $\hat{v}_t$ are, again, the OLS residuals of the unbiasedness regression).[17]

IV. THE TEST RESULTS

A. Tests of Unbiasedness

Tables 1.2 and 1.3 present regressions of actual spot depreciation (s_{t+k} - s_t) on forecasted depreciation ($E_t s_{t+k}$ - s_t). Rationality requires that the coefficient on forecasted depreciation be one, the constant be zero, and the disturbances be innovations with respect to the complete set of information available at time t. Tryon (1979) shows that using the change in the spot rate, rather than the level, constitutes a more stringent test of rational expectations. The 'first-difference' test of unbiasedness is to estimate the regression coefficients in (6):

$$s_{t+k} - s_t = a_0 + a_1(E_t s_{t+k} - s_t) + v_{t,k}$$

Adding the current spot, s_t, to both sides and rearranging terms we obtain:

$$s_{t+k} = a_0 + a_1 E_t s_{t+k} + (1-a_1)s_t + v_{t,k}$$

The first-difference regression, by explicitly including the current spot rate in the regression, allows us to distinguish whether it is the current spot rate or the forecast that actually has predictive power.

These tables show unbiasedness rejected at the .01 level for all equations except the one-month-ahead \$/Yen regression, which almost rejects at the .05 level. The slope coefficients, a_1, are particularly striking. In the short-horizon equations a_1 is generally positive, and close to zero, for all but the one-week-ahead \$/Yen equation. In the longer-horizon equations a_1 is generally negative, and close to -.5, implying that forecasters over-predicted the size of spot depreciation, and also got the direction of the exchange rate movements wrong. Further, across both short- and long-horizon equations, a_1 is insignificantly different from zero for all but the one-week-ahead \$/Yen equation. This suggests that the forecasts do no better than the contemporaneous spot in predicting future spot rate changes.

Figures 1.1 through 1.16 present graphs of MMS predicted and actual spot depreciation for the four currencies over four forecast horizons. A number of empirical regularities are notable. First, in all cases the variance of *ex post* depreciation (appreciation) was markedly greater than predicted changes. Second, the short-horizon forecasts generally predicted very small changes relative to the longer-horizon forecasts.[18] Both the one-week and two-week-ahead forecast error variances were found to be smaller than the one-month and three-month-ahead forecast error variances[19]. Third, the three-month-ahead forecasts from January 1983 through October 1984 consistently predict depreciation of between one and two percent for the four currencies, while, throughout the sample period, the actual spot rate appreciated by as much as six percent in some three-month periods. And, fourth, the one-month-ahead forecasts consistently predicted appreciation from October 1984 until August 1985, while actual spot depreciation began in March 1985 for the four currencies. Since October 1985, the one-month-ahead forecasts have been much closer aligned to actual spot movements.

Why did the three-month-ahead forecasts consistently predict depreciation in 1983-1984, while the actual spot rate continued to appreciate? Why did one-month-ahead forecasts not begin predicting depreciation until late summer 1985? A few explanations are possible. First, the MMS forecasts may be consistent with a "rational" Bayesian learning process model. After four years of appreciation, one-month-ahead forecasts of appreciation in early 1985 may have reflected a skepticism that the exchange rate would reverse itself so quickly. The new "depreciation regime" may not have been fully legitimized until the September 1985 G-5 meeting where a policy of dollar weakening was officially sanctioned. Further, if the forecasters perceived shifts in the exchange process over the estimation sample, the underlying covariance matrix estimator assumption--that changes in the exchange rate are ergodic (every sequence is equally representative of the whole process) may not be justified, in which case the standard errors presented in Table 1.3 may be suspect. This explanation is, however, less convincing for the earlier sample three-month-ahead forecasts, which consistently predicted depreciation after two years of consistent, albeit volatile, spot appreciation.

A second explanation for the biased forecasts, which has been widely discussed in the literature, is the peso problem: the existence of a small probability of a large depreciation which did not occur over the sample period used (Krasker (1980)). The forecasters may have rationally incorporated the true probability of depreciation in their predictions, but, because the three-month-ahead forecast sample ended before the spot rate began to depreciate, the test statistics are able to reject unbiasedness.

Dornbusch (1985) states that if we think of the dollar appreciation as a single rational speculative bubble (where the small probability event is the bursting of the bubble)[20] this probability should have been fully incorporated in the interest differential paid on dollar assets. While the interest differential did rise sharply after 1980 (when the dollar began its appreciation), both long and short-term interest differentials declined after mid-1984, and yet the actual and forecasted dollar continued to appreciate through February 1985. Frankel (1985) shows that the short-term interest differential was insufficient to sustain a rational dollar bubble between January 1985 and March 1985. He finds that the cumulative probability of noncollapse over this period would have been only three percent.

A final explanation for the survey expectations may well be that the forecasts are biased, that forecasters over-weighted the small probability of depreciation in their three-month-ahead forecasts and under-weighted the probability of depreciation in their one-month forecasts.

B. Tests of Weak- and Strong-Form RE

The second type of RE test examines whether expectations incorporate available information. As a preliminary check for weak-form RE, the Durbin-Watson statistic on the previously presented non-overlapping short-horizon unbiasedness tests do not suggest the presence of serial correlation in the regression forecast errors for all but the one-week-ahead $/Yen equation. A direct check for serial correlation involves regressing the current period forecast error on the previous period error (equation (4) presented earlier). Table 1.4 presents the forecast error regression results; a significant slope coefficient would indicate that forecasters did not incorporate past errors in their current forecast.

While three of the two-week-horizon equations show significant constant terms, all equations show insignificant serial correlation. This indicates that although the short-horizon forecasts were generally biased, they did efficiently incorporate information from past errors. For the one-month and three-month-ahead cases, since the previous forecast errors are not available before the next forecast, an analogous test is not feasible.

The one- and three-month-ahead forward rates provide strong-form tests of rationality. Since the MMS survey is taken after 12pm EST; the noon N.Y. forward rate is available to forecasters. Table 1.5 presents the estimated regression results of the MMS forecast error on the appropriately aligned one- and three-month-ahead forward premium ($f_{t,k}$ - s_t).

These regression results indicate that the forward premium contains additional information for the three-month-ahead forecasts. While the $/DM one-month-ahead forecast also fails the test of efficiency, it is the constant term, not the forward premium, that leads to the rejection. The three-month-ahead forward rates over the early sample period generally (wrongly) predicted spot depreciation, as did the survey predictions (but by a smaller percentage). The one-month-ahead forward rates predicted spot depreciation throughout the later sample period. The MMS appreciation forecasts were, therefore, more correct for the first five months of the sample. The forward rate then "beat" the MMS forecasts through August 1985, as the survey continued to predict appreciation incorrectly. After September 1985 the survey correctly predicted larger depreciation than did the one-month forward rate.

V. SUMMARY AND CONCLUSIONS

This chapter tests the rational expectations hypothesis in foreign exchange markets using a newly available set of survey data collected by Money Market Services. Tests examine whether these expectations series are unbiased and whether they incorporate information available from past forecast errors and the forward rate.

The estimation procedure used on overlapping data allows both for conditional heteroskedasticity and for serially correlated forecast errors. Seemingly unrelated regressions are used in tests of the short-horizon non-overlapping data. The test results indicate that the MMS forecasts consistently fail to predict future changes in the spot rate. Indeed, the MMS forecasts do no better than the current spot rate in forecasting the future spot rate. In change form, all forecasts are biased, and the three-month-ahead MMS forecasts were found to violate strong-form RE.

There are a number of possible explanations of the behavior of the survey forecasts. It is possible that, despite the apparent rejection of unbiasedness, the early sample period was not long enough to bear out the forecasters' "rational" expectation of depreciation. However, rationality arguments, whether in the context of a bayesian or bubble process, do not seem convincing, given the direction and magnitude of forecast errors over the two sample periods.

Finally, it seems that there is a great deal to be learned from subjecting survey data on expectations to rigorous tests. This is particularly so for high-quality data covering the expectations of expert participants in asset markets. Further work with the MMS and similar data should, therefore, generate additional useful perspectives on exchange rate behavior.[21]

TABLE 1.1

Tests for Forecast Error Conditional Homoskedasticity

Results of conditional homoskedasticity tests on three- and one-month-ahead survey forecast errors. Step 1, regresses actual spot depreciation on expected depreciation.

$$s_{t+k} - s_t = a_0 + a_1(E_t s_{t+k} - s_t) + v_{t,k}$$

Step 2 regresses the square of the forecast error from step 1 on expected depreciation and the same variable squared for the four countries.

$$\hat{v}^2_{t,k} = b_0 + b_1(E_t s_{t+k} - s_t) + b_2(E_t s_{t+k} - s_t)^2 + \zeta_{t,k}$$

k=4,12 (weeks). The square of the forecast error should be constant with respect to all instruments available at time t; the χ^2 statistic pertains to the joint hypothesis that $b_1=b_2=0$; * denotes rejection of the joint hypothesis at the .05 level.

currency	horizon	smpl	$\chi^2(2)$
\$/STLG	3-month	83-84	1.58
	1-month	84-86	5.71*
\$/DM	3-month	83-84	1.31
	1-month	84-86	1.10
\$/SWF	3-month	83-84	1.56
	1-month	84-86	1.82
\$/YEN	3-month	83-84	0.77
	1-month	84-86	6.40*

TABLE 1.2

Unbiasedness Tests on Short Horizon Forecasts

Regressions of actual two- and one-week spot rate depreciation on forecasted depreciation.

$$s_{t+k} - s_t = a_0 + a_1(E_t s_{t+k} - s_t) + v_{t,k}$$

k=1,2 (week). The numbers in parentheses are the estimated standard errors of the coefficients; * denotes rejection at the .05 level and ** at the .01 level for the hypotheses that $a_0=0$ and $a_1=1$. The χ^2 statistic pertains to the joint hypothesis that $a_0=0$ and $a_1=1$.

currency	k	smpl	a_0	a_1	D.W.	R^2	$\chi^2(2)$
$/STLG	2-WK	83-84	-.005 (.003)*	.034 (.119)**	1.99	.003	96.2**
	1-WK	84-86	.001 (.003)	-.171 (.181)**	1.85	.05	44.3**
$/DM	2-WK	83-84	-.004 (.002)*	.122 (.095)**	1.79	.03	155.3**
	1-WK	84-86	.002 (.003)	.049 (.137)**	1.85	.01	48.8**
$/SWF	2-WK	83-84	-.004 (.002)*	.101 (.091)**	1.80	.01	84.0**
	1-WK	84-86	.002 (.003)	.064 (.118)**	1.88	.01	62.3**
$/YEN	2-WK	83-84	-.001 (.002)	.166 (.100)**	2.05	.02	69.3**
	1-WK	84-86	.003 (.002)	.502 (.146)**	1.59	.07	12.8**

TABLE 1.3

Unbiasedness Tests on Long Horizon Forecasts

Regressions of actual three- and one-month spot rate depreciation on forecasted depreciation.

$$s_{t+k} - s_t = a_0 + a_1(E_t s_{t+k} - s_t) + v_{t,k}$$

k=4,12 (week). The numbers in parentheses are the estimated standard errors of the coefficients; * denotes rejection at the .05 level and ** at the .01 level for the hypotheses that $a_0=0$ and $a_1=1$. MA is the moving average assumption for the disturbances. The χ^2 statistic pertains to the joint hypothesis that $a_0=0$ and $a_1=1$.

currency	k	smpl	a_0	a_1	MA	R^2	$\chi^2(2)$
$/STLG	3-MO	83-84	-.029 (.015)*	-.450 (.395)**	5	.01	39.23**
	1-MO	84-86	-.001 (.006)	-.505 (.329)**	1	.05	21.44**
$/DM	3-MO	83-84	-.043 (.016)**	.412 (.529)	5	.01	23.26**
	1-MO	84-86	.014 (.007)	-.248 (.392)**	1	.01	15.07**
$/SWF	3-MO	83-84	-.033 (.009)**	.054 (.099)**	5	.001	135.38**
	1-MO	84-86	.012 (.008)	-.374 (.425)**	1	.02	11.52**
$/YEN	3-MO	83-84	.003 (.016)	-.457 (.626)**	5	.02	9.38**
	1-MO	84-86	.015 (.008)	.341 (.359)	1	.01	4.98

TABLE 1.4
Weak-Form Rational Expectations Tests

Regressions of the current period forecast error on the previous period forecast error.

$$s_{t+k} - E_t s_{t+k} = \beta_0 + \beta_1(s_t - E_{t-k}s_t) + \eta_{t,k}$$

k=1,2 (week). The numbers in parentheses are the estimated standard errors of the coefficients; * denotes rejection at the .05 level and ** at the .01 level for the hypotheses that $\beta_0=0$ and $\beta_1=0$. The χ^2 statistic pertains to the joint hypothesis that $\beta_0=\beta_1=0$.

currency	k	smpl	β_0	β_1	D.H.	R^2	$\chi^2(2)$
$/STLG	2-WK	83-84	.004 (.003)*	-.050 (.122)	.093	.002	3.43
	1-WK	84-86	-.005 (.004)	-.033 (.053)	.181	.001	1.85
$/DM	2-WK	83-84	.007 (.003)**	.008 (.086)	-.174	.001	6.31*
	1-WK	84-86	-.002 (.003)	-.025 (.034)	.303	.001	1.07
$/SWF	2-WK	83-84	.008 (.002)**	-.003 (.012)	.132	.001	10.09**
	1-WK	84-86	-.001 (.003)	-.003 (.008)	.225	.001	0.29
$/YEN	2-WK	83-84	.003 (.002)	.124 (.090)	-.739	.014	4.85
	1-WK	84-86	-.002 (.002)	.129 (.082)	.705	.001	3.64

TABLE 1.5

Strong-Form Rational Expectations Tests

Regressions of the MMS forecast error on the appropriately aligned three- and one-month-ahead forward premium.

$$(s_{t+k} - s_t) - (E_t s_{t+k} - s_t) = \delta_0 + \delta_1 (f_{t,k} - s_t) + \epsilon_{t,k}$$

k=4,12 (week). The numbers in parentheses are the estimated standard errors of the coefficients; * denotes rejection at the .05 level and ** at the .01 level for the hypotheses that $\delta_0=0$ and $\delta_1=0$. MA is the moving average assumption for the disturbances. The value of the χ^2 statistic pertains to the test of the joint hypothesis that $\delta_0=\delta_1=0$.

currency	k	smpl	δ_0	δ_1	MA	R^2	$\chi^2(2)$
$/STLG	3-MO	83-84	-.039	-7.89	5	.37	128.8**
			(.006)**	(1.03)**			
	1-MO	84-86	.012	-1.26	1	.03	5.9
			(.017)	(1.56)			
$/DM	3-MO	83-84	.003	-4.96	5	.08	36.9**
			(.053)	(4.33)			
	1-MO	84-86	.019	-1.14	1	.03	6.4*
			(.008)**	(1.18)			
$/SWF	3-MO	83-84	.065	-7.89	5	.26	69.4**
			(.049)	(3.19)**			
	1-MO	84-86	.015	-1.15	1	.05	3.5
			(.009)	(1.11)			
$/YEN	3-MO	83-84	.003	-3.26	5	.06	6.9*
			(.035)	(3.59)			
	1-MO	84-86	.015	-.357	1	.01	3.1
			(.008)	(.783)			

FIGURE 1.1

2-WK $/STLG MMS AND ACTUAL DEPRECIATION

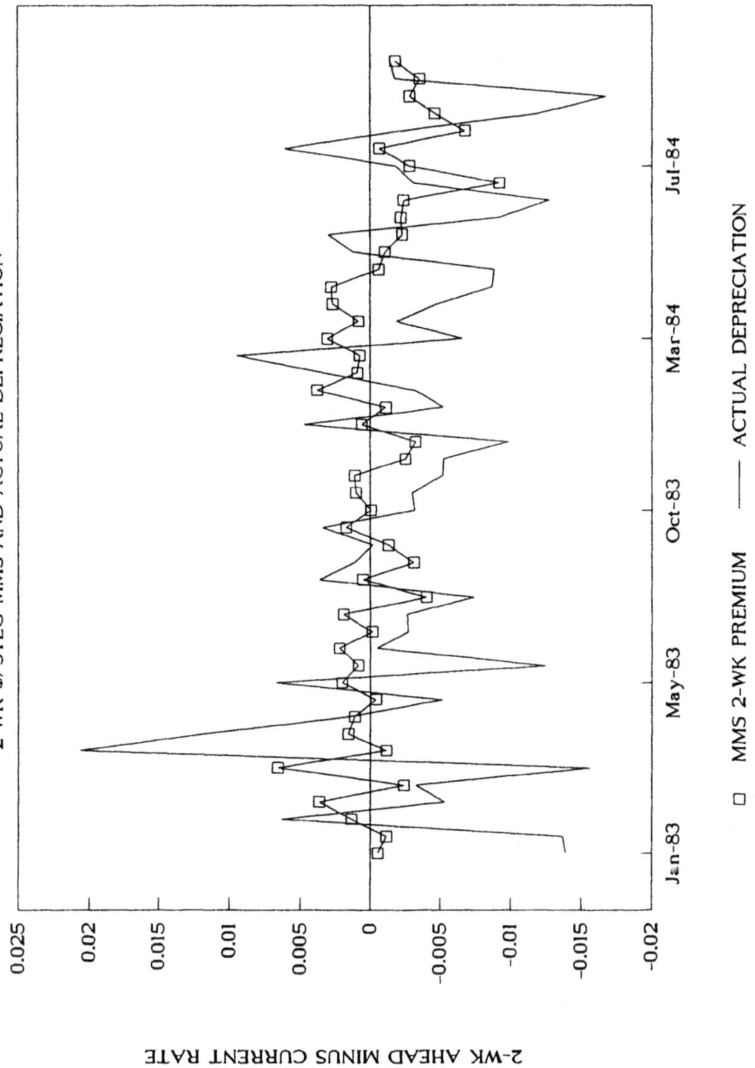

FIGURE 1.2

2-WK \$/DM MMS AND ACTUAL DEPRECIATION

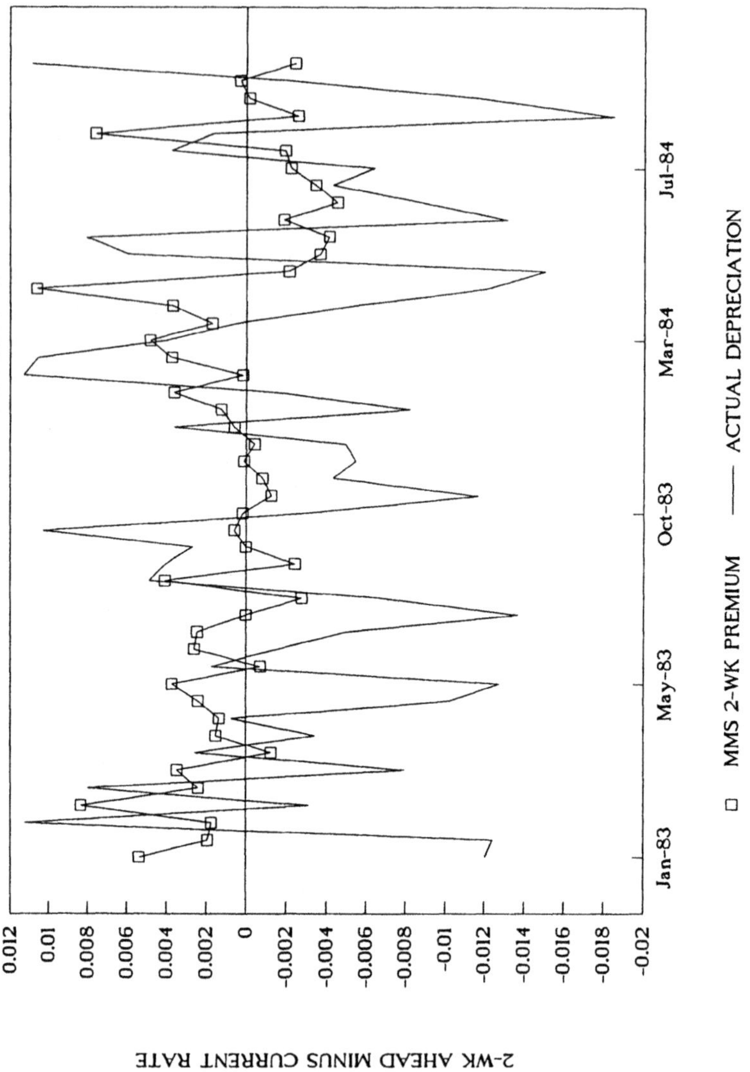

FIGURE 1.3

2-WK $/SWF MMS AND ACTUAL DEPRECIATION

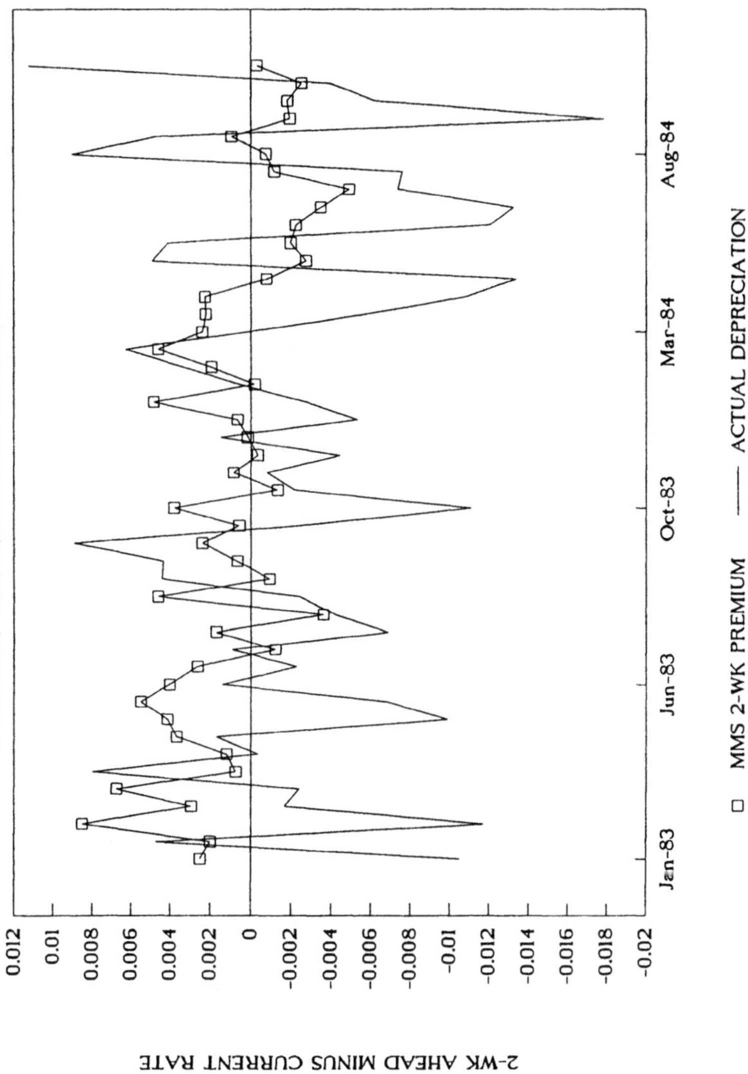

FIGURE 1.4

2-WK $/YEN MMS AND ACTUAL DEPRECIATION

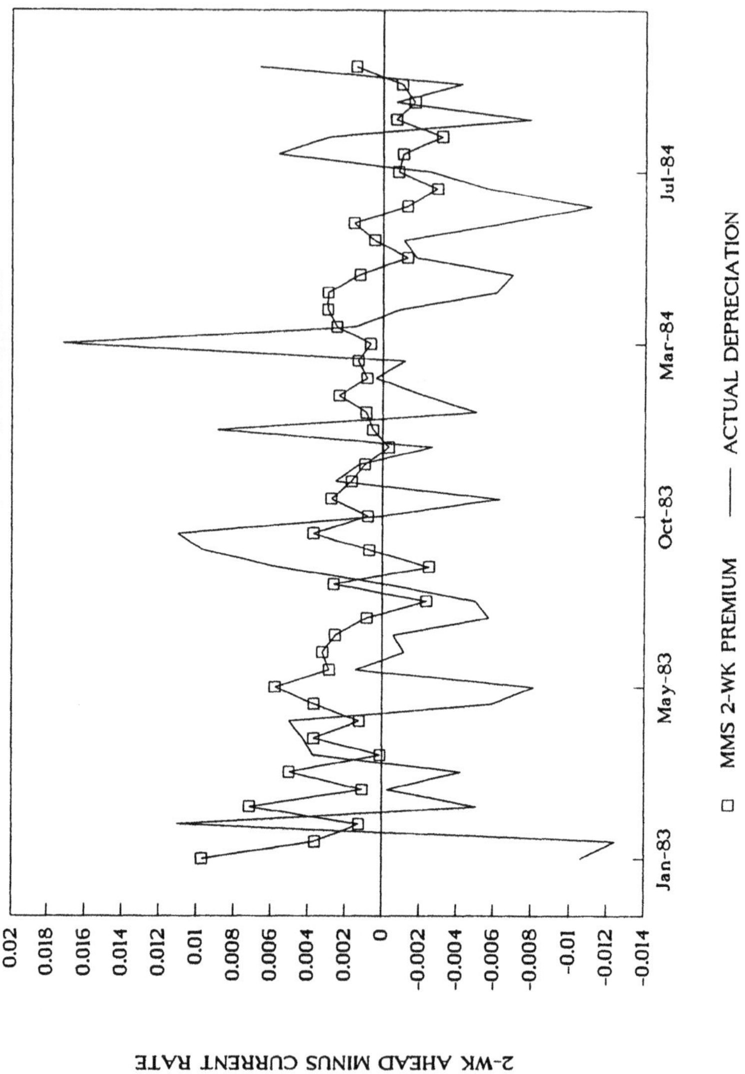

FIGURE 1.5

3-MO $/STLG MMS AND ACTUAL DEPRECIATION

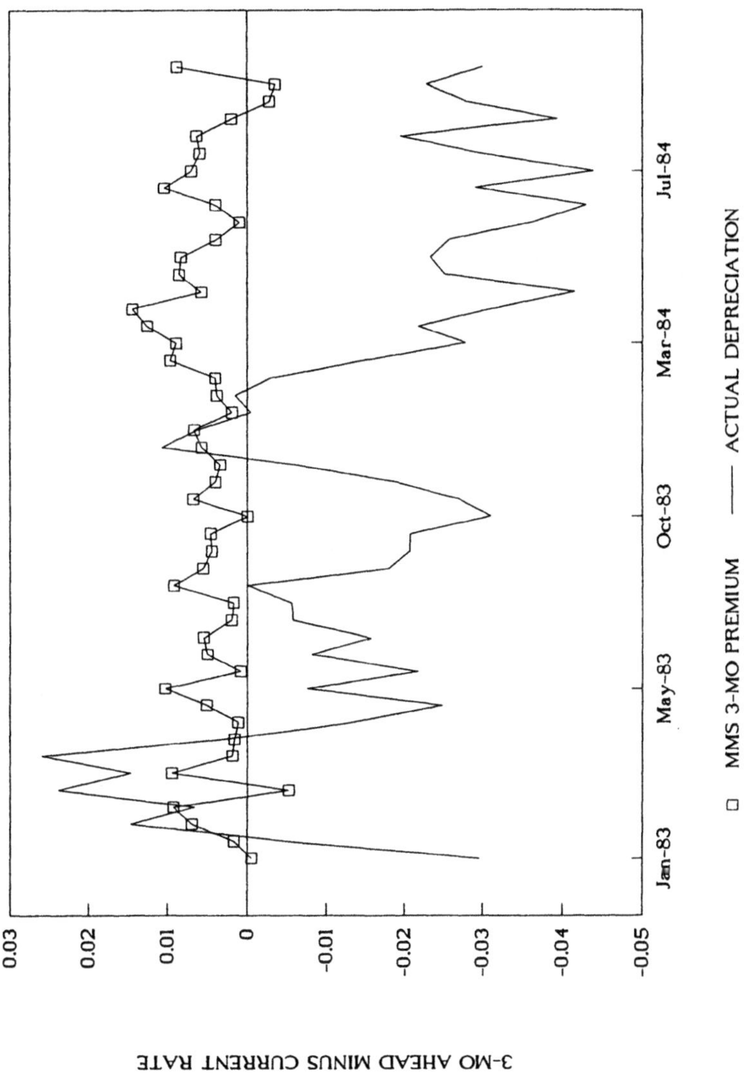

FIGURE 1.6

3-MO $/DM MMS AND ACTUAL DEPRECIATION

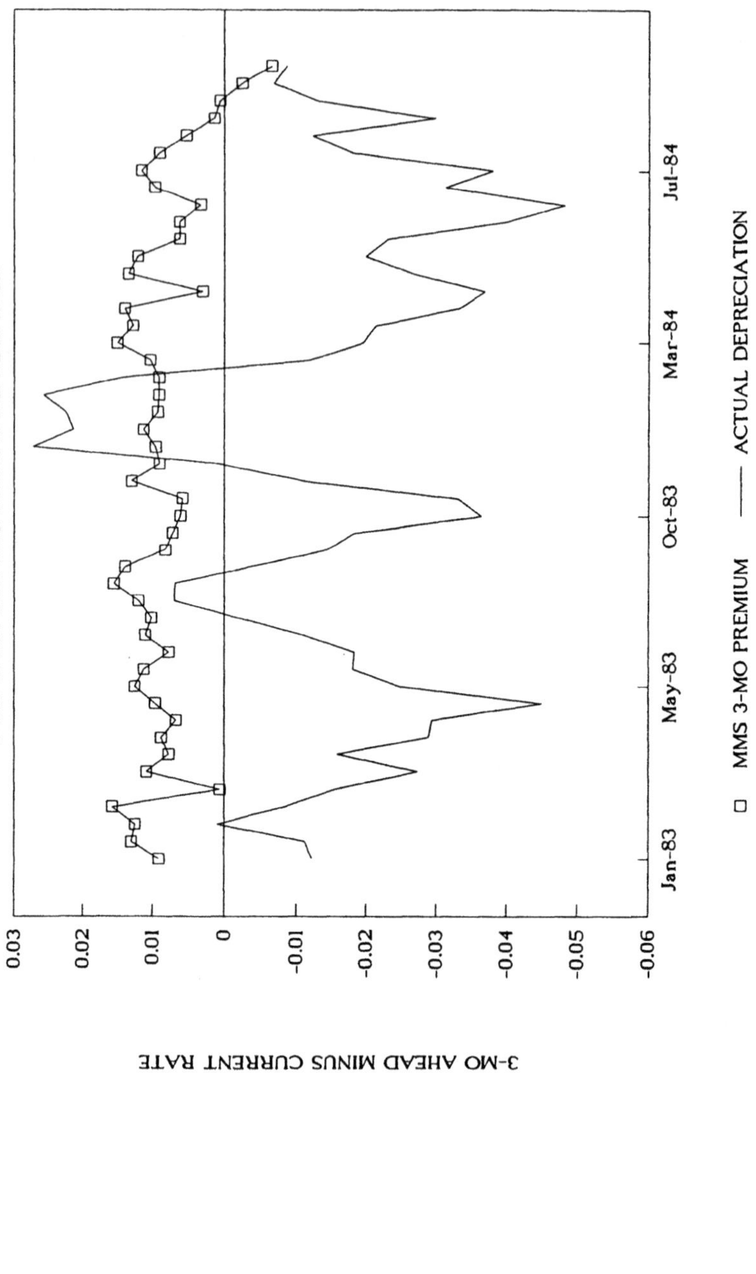

FIGURE 1.7

3-MO $/SWF MMS AND ACTUAL DEPRECIATION

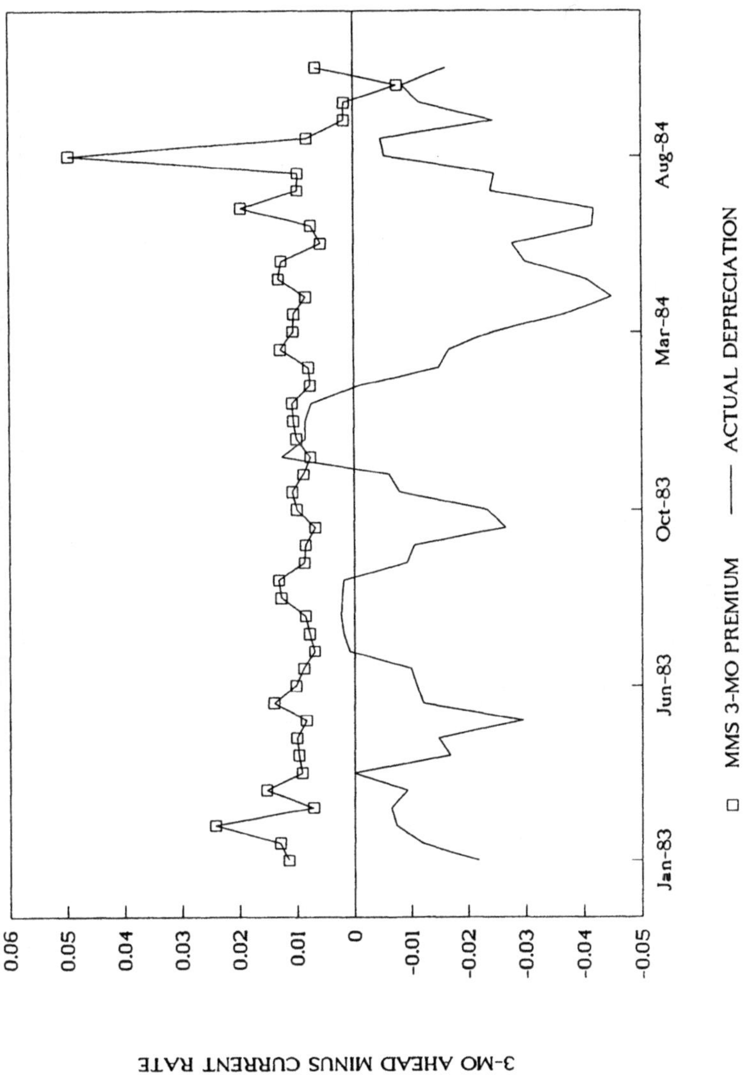

FIGURE 1.8

3-MO $/YEN MMS AND ACTUAL DEPRECIATION

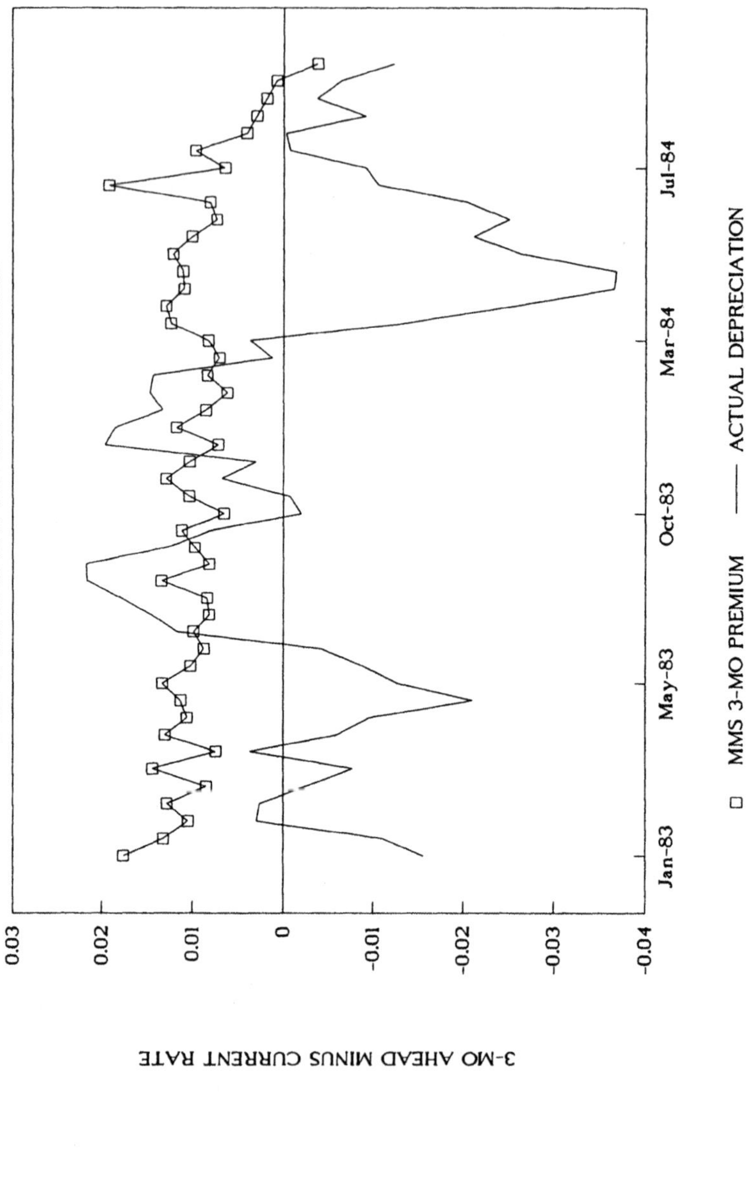

FIGURE 1.9

1-WK $/STLG MMS AND ACTUAL DEPRECIATION

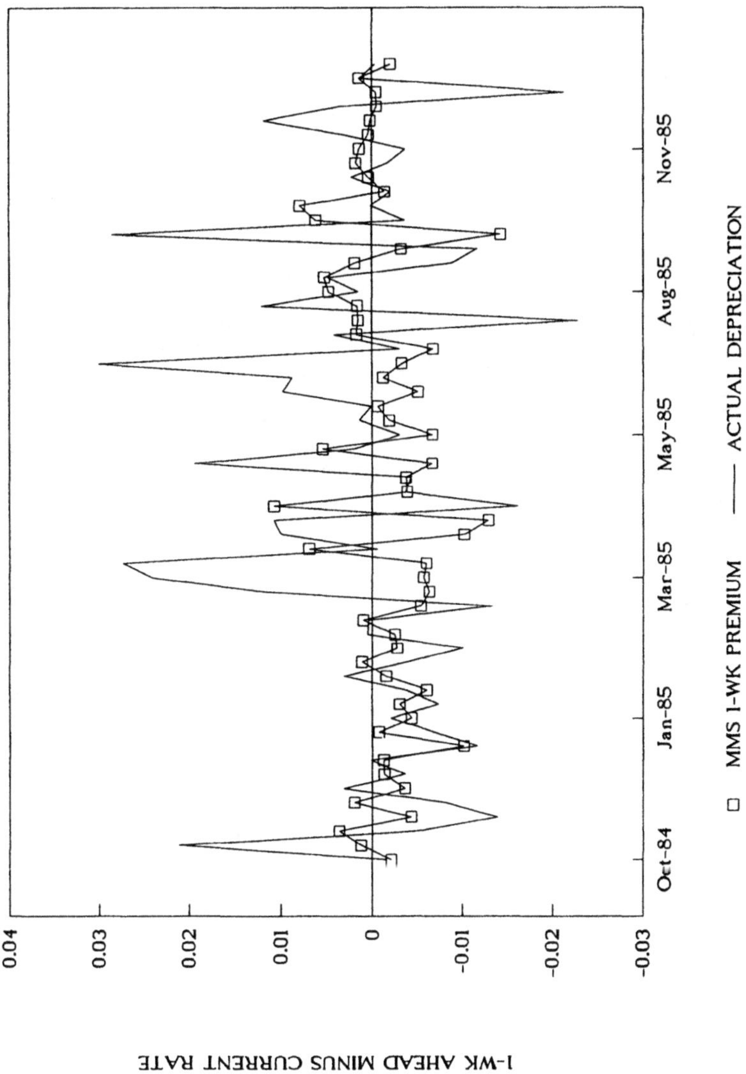

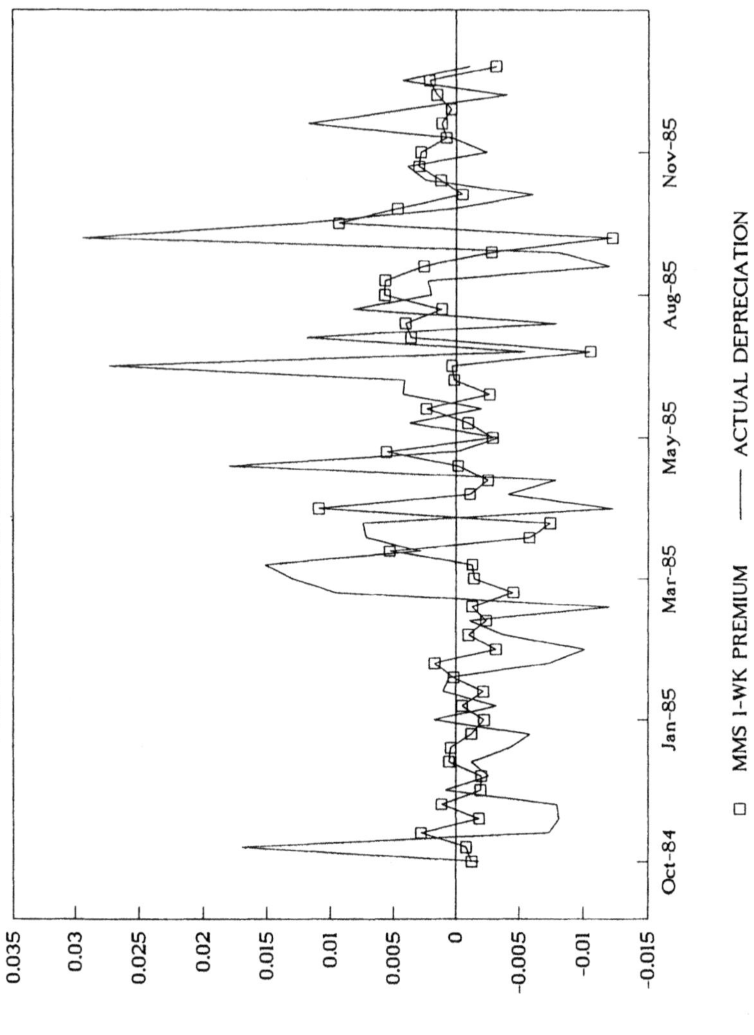

FIGURE 1.10

1-WK $/DM MMS AND ACTUAL DEPRECIATION

FIGURE 1.11

1-WK $/SWF MMS AND ACTUAL DEPRECIATION

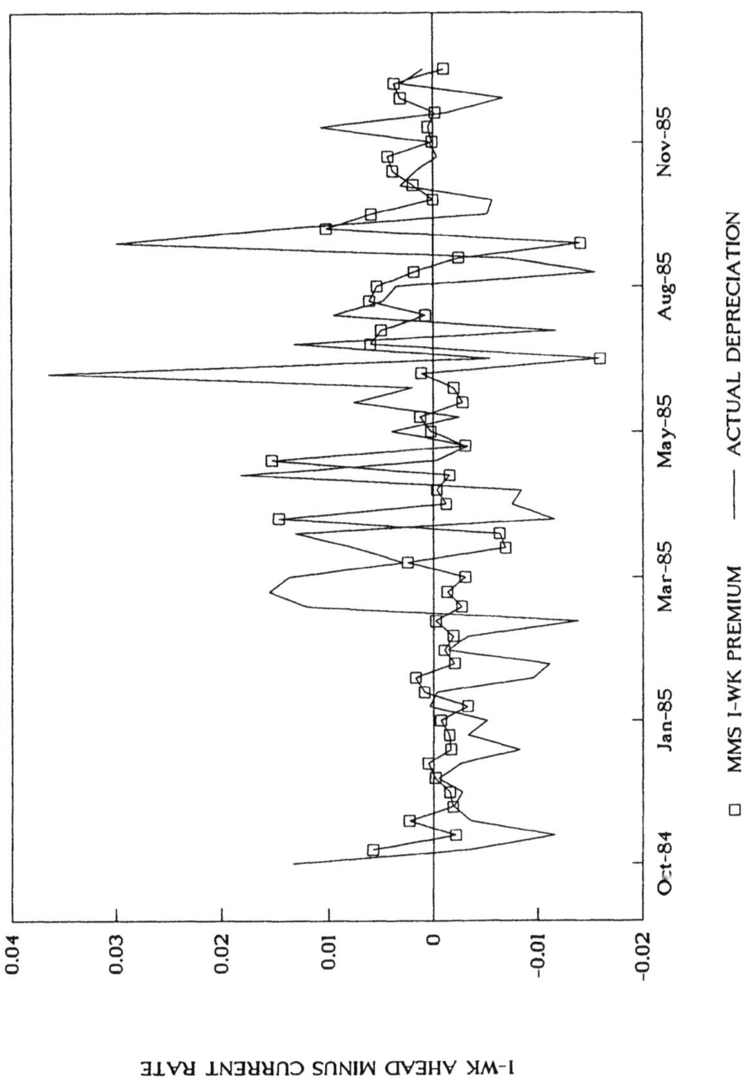

FIGURE 1.12

1-WK $/YEN MMS AND ACTUAL DEPRECIATION

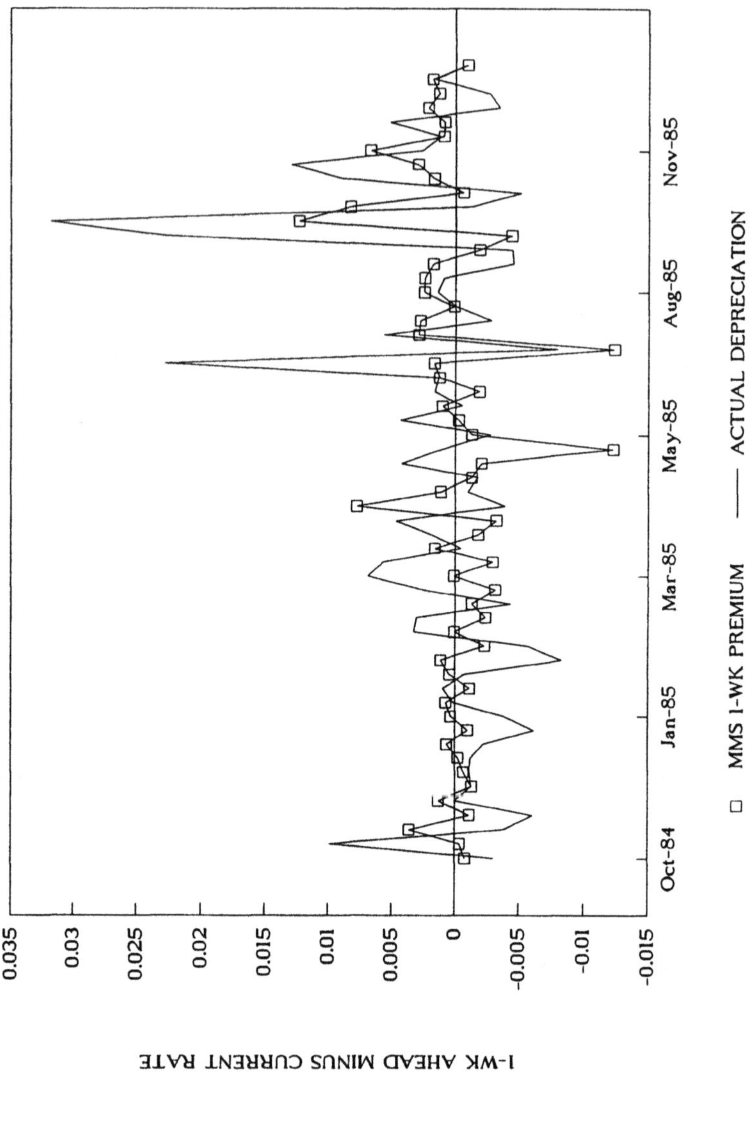

FIGURE 1.13

1-MO $/STLG MMS AND ACTUAL DEPRECIATION

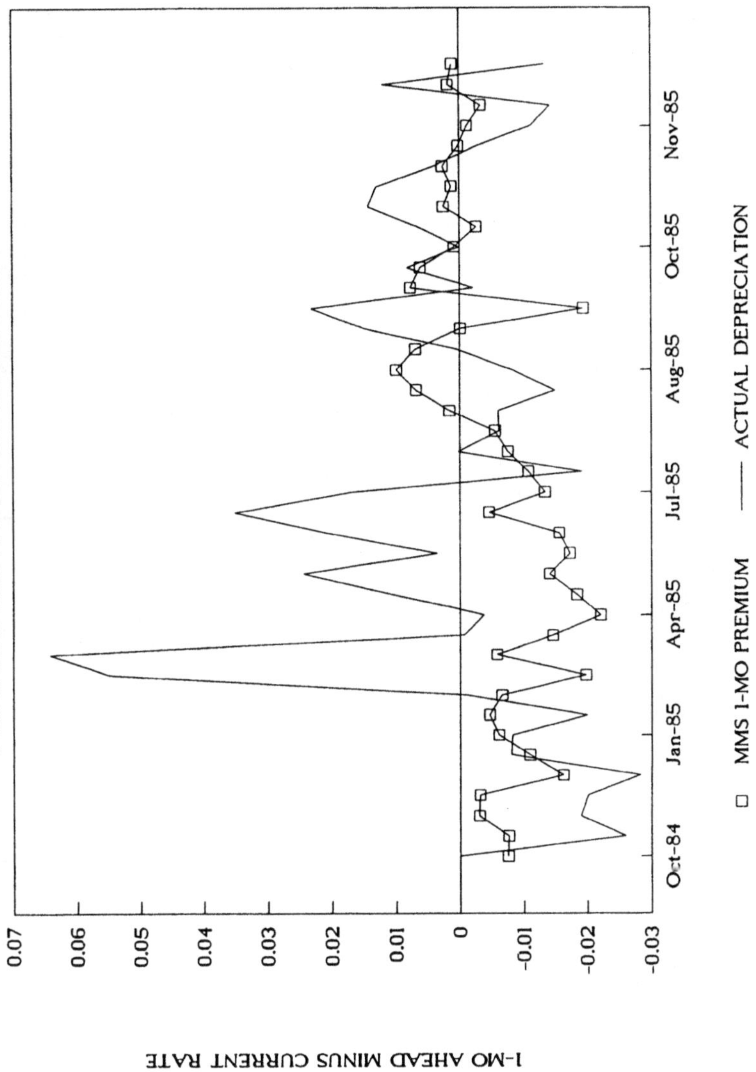

FIGURE 1.14

1-MO $/DM MMS AND ACTUAL DEPRECIATION

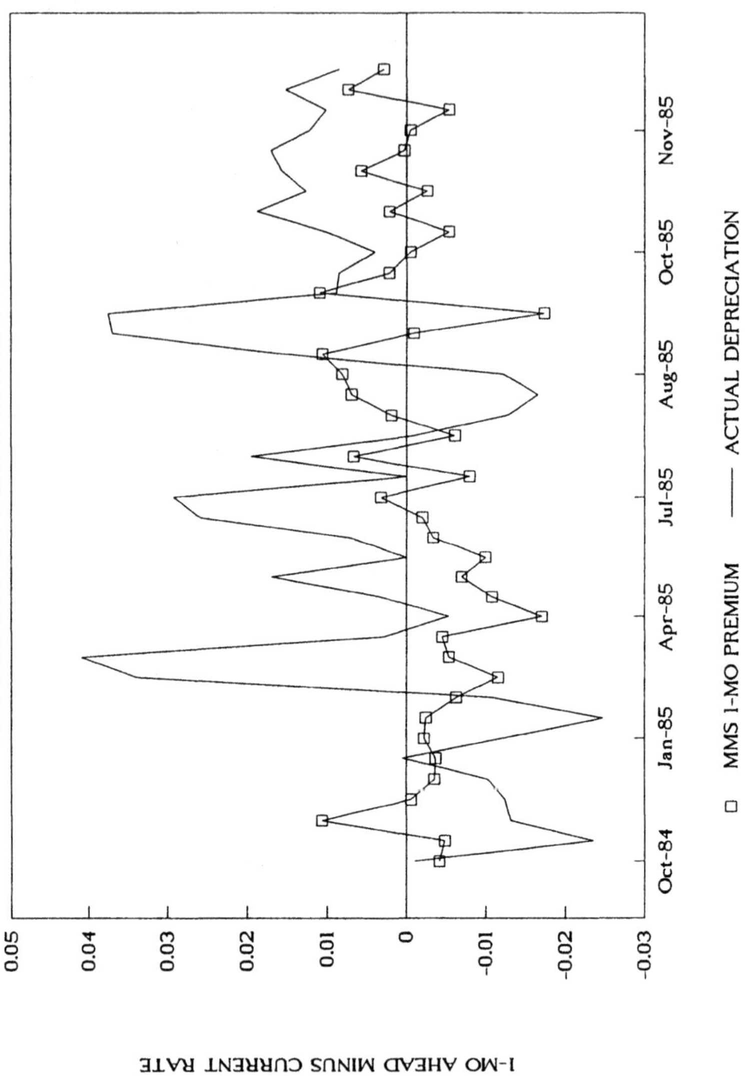

FIGURE 1.15

1-MO $/SWF MMS AND ACTUAL DEPRECIATION

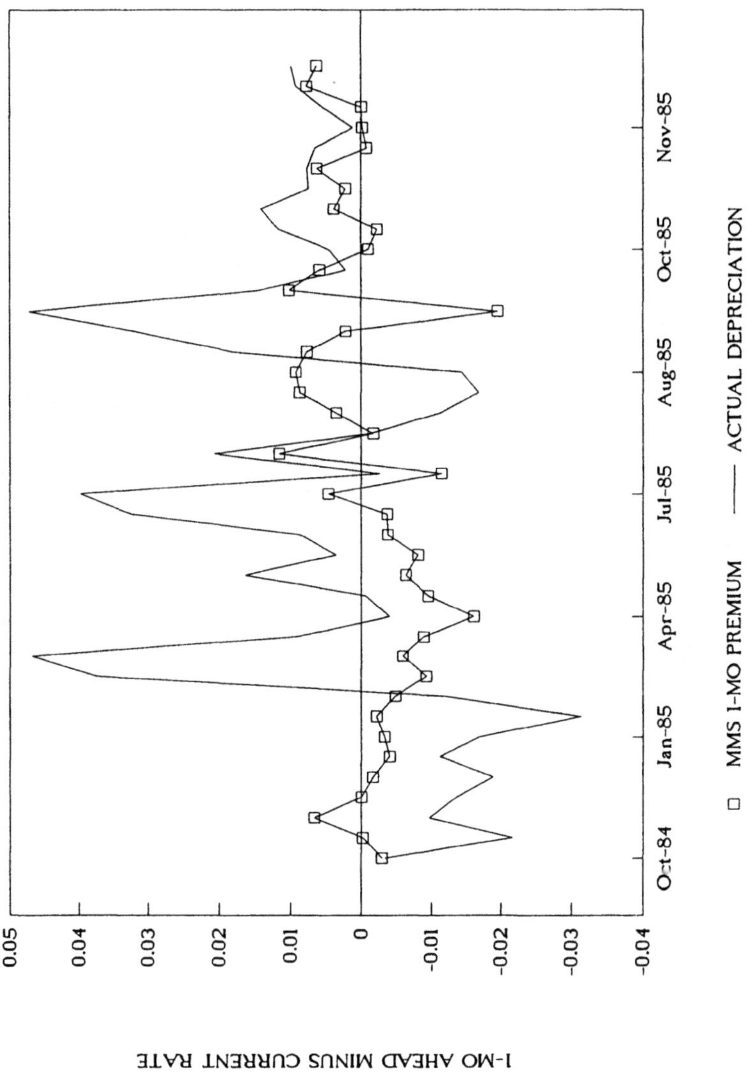

FIGURE 1.16

1-MO $/YEN MMS AND ACTUAL DEPRECIATION

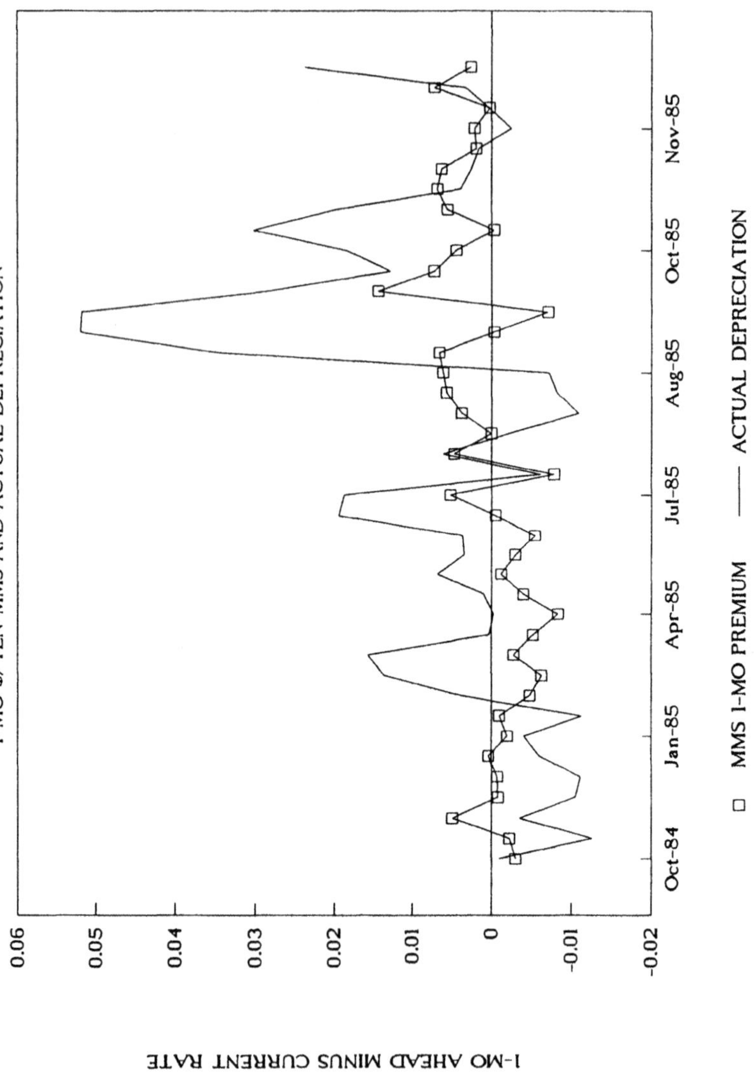

NOTES

1. Muth (1961) defined a rational expectation as "own-model-consistent." This definition requires that there be a specific model which agents both know and use to formulate their expectations. Typically, however, tests of rationality are not based on a specific model but require that the prediction error be uncorrelated with "all available information."

2. I thank Mark Porter and David Broder from MMS for providing the survey data.

3. Seminal papers on the topic include: Friedman (1953) and Johnson (1969).

4. See Appendix A for an example of the fundamental variables typically included in equilibrium exchange rate models and the central role the expectations formation process plays in such models.

5. See, for example, Frenkel (1976), Branson, Halttunen, and Mason (1979), Hooper and Morton (1982), Edison (1985).

6. Because an exchange rate for one country is the reciprocal of the exchange rate for the other country, by Jensen's inequality it will not generally be true that both the expected value of the future spot rate *and* its reciprocal are equal to the forward rate and the reciprocal of the forward rate, respectively. This is known as Siegal's (1972) paradox. The forward rate will, therefore, be a combination of the expected future spot rate, possibly a risk premium, and a convexity term arising from Siegal's paradox. McCulloch (1975) finds that the latter term, although important in principle, is empirically trivial.

7. Hansen and Hodrick (1983) and Hodrick and Srivastava (1984) provide weak evidence in support of a time varying risk premium, using a single-beta latent variable model. Domowitz and Hakkio (1985) find little evidence of the existence of a risk premium based on the conditional variance of market forecast errors, which are assumed to follow an ARCH process.

8. See, for example, Tryon (1979), Hansen and Hodrick (1980), Hakkio (1981), Cumby and Obstfeld (1981, 1984) and Hsieh (1984).

9. See, for example, Akerlof and Yellen (1985), Haltiwagner and Waldman (1985).

10. Numerous papers have examined this bi-annual data set on inflation forecasts compiled by Joseph Livingston of the *Philadelphia Inquirer.* See, for example, Carlson (1977) for tests of unbiasedness and efficiency. Struth (1984) finds that a simple Kalman filter using only past price information can out-perform the Livingston forecasts.

11. An early version of Frankel and Froot (1987) and Froot (1985) use a semi-annual mail survey published by Amex Bank Review and the Economist Financial Report to examine exchange rate expectations. Although their results are consistent with this chapter's findings, the fact that the respondents were not polled simultaneously, and that the number of survey dates was small, may greatly reduce the power of their tests.

12. In the strictest sense, the forecast errors should be regressed on "all available information" to test for rationality. In the interest of parameter parsimony, however, only those variables that models would predict to influence exchange rates are generally included.

13. This, more specifically, tests only that the forecast error, $(s_{t+k}-E_t s_{t+k})$ is white noise, not that it is an innovation with respect to $(s_t, E_{t-1}s_t, \ldots)$.

14. In order to avoid Siegel's (1972) Paradox (which arises because the expectation of an inverse does not, in general, equal one over the expectation of the original variable), spot, forward and survey expectations are in logarithms, thereby ensuring that results are independent of whether exchange rates are expressed in units of home or foreign currency.

15. MMS publishes the median (rather than the mean) forecast to its clients. The thirty individual forecasts per survey are not, in general, symmetrically distributed. If a distribution is symmetric the mean will equal the median but, if not, the median measure gives distributional outliers less influence than does the mean.

16. Forward contracts are set for the same date however many months ahead, (i.e., Jan. 1 to Feb. 1 for an one-month contract) but delivery takes place two business days later (one day for Canada). However, unless the trader is holding a covered position, she must cover the short-term position since spot transactions also take two business days. This chapter assumes that forward contracts are uncovered, so that spot rates are aligned two days before actual delivery of the forward contract.

17. These estimates were done with RATS software (VAR Econometrics) using the MCOV instruction.

18. Discussions with MMS indicate that the survey changed from two-week and three-month-ahead forecasts to one-week and one-month-ahead forecasts specifically because the forecasters felt more comfortable reporting shorter-horizon forecasts.

19. In contrast, Engle and Kraft (1983) show, in another context, that forecast error variances estimated from ARCH models for several periods ahead can be less than one period inflation forecast error variances.

20. The probability of depreciation might be based on the fact that fundamentals (see Appendix A for examples) were stacked against the dollar by mid-1984, or could represent a response to record U.S. budget deficits over the sample three years.

21. The MMS survey data on exchange rate expectations have subsequently been examined in numerous studies, most notably Dominguez and Frankel (1992a,b), Frankel and Froot (1987, 1990a,b), and Froot and Frankel (1989). Analysis of exchange rate expectations in the late 1980s largely confirm the results that were found for the early 1980s; the hypothesis of rational expectations is decisively rejected. In a related study, Ito (1990) finds evidence of heterogenous irrationality in a panel series of survey data compiled by the JCIF in Tokyo.

CHAPTER 2

The Informational Role of Official Foreign Exchange Intervention Policy: The Signalling Hypothesis

I. INTRODUCTION

After the breakdown of the Bretton Woods system in March 1973, most economists predicted that central bank intervention in foreign exchange markets would diminish dramatically. This did not, however, turn out to be the case. Evidence suggests that the use of official foreign exchange intervention actually increased under flexible exchange rates (Frenkel (1978), Dooley (1979)). Moreover, most central banks, as matters of policy, claim that they sterilize their intervention operations. If this is true, then they offset their foreign currency transactions with open-market operations, leaving the monetary base unchanged.

The continued use of sterilized intervention has been puzzling for two reasons. First, it is unclear what central banks hope to accomplish by intervening in currency markets in a floating rate regime. The most popular explanation has been that banks intervene to "lean against the wind," attempting to smooth and thereby stabilize exchange rate fluctuations. But there is no theoretical reason that exchange rate fluctuations should need smoothing. Indeed, if a central bank slows an exchange rate that is moving toward its equilibrium trend, leaning-against-the-wind would be destabilizing (Wonnacott (1982)).

The second puzzle concerning sterilized intervention is whether such intervention can ever influence the path of exchange rates. Theory suggests that intervention should have little if any real effect. In the context of standard monetary models of exchange rate determination, sterilized intervention has no effect, because it leaves the monetary base unchanged. In some portfolio balance models of exchange rate determination, in which foreign and domestic assets are imperfect substitutes, sterilized intervention may be effective if it alters the worldwide asset mix sufficiently to induce portfolio rebalancing (Kouri and Porter (1974), Girton and Henderson (1977), and Branson (1979)).[1] However, in other portfolio balance models that allow for intergenerational transfers, sterilized intervention is not effective (Stockman (1979), Obstfeld (1980)). Moreover, empirical evidence suggests that the change in relative asset stocks necessary to induce a change in relative asset prices is probably larger than typical intervention operations (Dooley and Isard (1982), Frankel (1982), Obstfeld (1983), Rogoff (1984)).

This chapter presents and tests an explanation for sterilized intervention that resolves both of these puzzles. Central banks may utilize sterilized intervention, not as an independent policy tool, but as a signal to the market of future monetary policy intentions. In this context, intervention may constitute a way for central banks to credibly transmit *inside* information to market participants. Central banks, however, also have the incentive to manipulate market expectations in order to pursue exchange rate targets that are inconsistent with future monetary policy. Market participants know this, and consequently do not always believe intervention signals.

I argue that the signalling hypothesis offers a convincing framework for viewing intervention policy. First, a signalling role provides a clear mechanism whereby sterilized intervention can have significant real effects. Neither the "budget constraint"[2] on the size of intervention, nor its lack of effect on the monetary base, should compromise its effectiveness. Second, the characteristics of intervention are consistent with the necessary conditions for a credible signal. In the context of standard financial signalling models (e.g., Ross (1977)), the determinant of intervention credibility should be a negative relationship between the accuracy of the signal and its cost to the central bank.

The empirical tests in this chapter were made possible by agreements with the Board of Governors of the Federal Reserve System and the West German Bundesbank in which both allowed the use of their daily data on official intervention in the foreign exchange market. A first set of empirical tests examines whether intervention is driven by the divergence between *inside* central bank information about the short-term path of the money supply, and the market's money supply expectations. This is the fundamental implication of the signalling hypothesis motive for intervention. If intervention is to transmit information to the market, it should be driven not by changes in the money supply *per se*, but by its unexpected component. A second set of tests examines the relationship between intervention and the path of exchange rates.

The evidence shows that this information divergence did indeed drive Fed intervention policy during the one recent period when the Fed was perceived as most credible by market participants--the aftermath of the shift to M1 targeting in October 1979. In other periods there is no consistent correspondence between this informational divergence and intervention policy. This implies that the Fed's motive for intervention shifts over time. Intervention is sometimes tied to future monetary policy (and if this is known, then intervention policy informs the market), but intervention at other times is unrelated to monetary policy. I conclude that in the later periods intervention may have been used for targeting purposes.

Section II of the chapter discusses the hypothesis that intervention is used to convey information to the market about future monetary policy. Section III presents two approaches to the problem of identifying when a central bank is credible. Sections IV and V present empirical tests of the signalling hypothesis and Section VI presents conclusions.

II. SIGNALLING, FED INFORMATION, AND FED CREDIBILITY

This section describes how central bank intervention can serve to signal future monetary policy intentions to the market. Part A discusses the signalling hypothesis in the context of the asset approach to exchange rate determination. Part B relates the signalling, or informational, motive for intervention to the problem of Fed credibility.

A. Fed Intervention as a Signal

There is a long history of informal thought about the notion that sterilized intervention might constitute a signal. Many authors, including Friedman (1953), Dooley (1979), Mussa (1981), Gensberg (1981), and Henderson (1984) have suggested that intervention may serve to communicate to the market the central bank's *inside* information about its own future monetary policy. The potential role played by intervention as a signalling instrument can be seen directly in the context of the asset approach to exchange rate determination. In these models, exchange rates are forward looking, and they are expectationally efficient with respect to public information. The current spot rate can be represented as

$$s_t = \frac{1}{1+\beta}\sum_{k=0}^{\infty}\left[\frac{\beta}{1+\beta}\right]^k E_t(z_{t+k}|\Omega_t) \tag{1}$$

where s_t is the current spot exchange rate in log form, β is the interest semi-elasticity of money demand, z_t is a vector of exogenous driving variables that include money and (real) income differentials between the two countries, and Ω_t is the public information set at time t. This equation shows that the current spot rate depends on current expectations, given the information set Ω_t, of all important driving variables (the z's) from now into the indefinite future.[3]

The potential signalling role of intervention derives from the fact that the central bank is known to have superior information about one of the driving variables--the future course of home money, m_{t+k}. If sterilized intervention is a function of future monetary policy, then by observing intervention, the market learns something about future m_{t+k}, which in turn, affects the market's expectations in (1) and so also exchange rates.[4]

Existing empirical literature suggests that there are potential efficiency gains to be derived from releasing Fed information to the market sooner, rather than later. Evidence indicates that spot rates jump at the time of announcements containing new information about the money supply and, inferentially, about the implications for future Fed policy (Cornell (1982), Engel and Frankel (1984), Hakkio and Pearce (1985)).[5] If the Fed sees some benefit in being "informational," in the sense of making the current exchange rate more accurately reflect current and future underlying economic conditions, then intervention can fill this role.

Sterilized intervention is uniquely suited to serving such an informational role in the market because, by definition, it is a policy commitment that the Fed can make that has no real effects on the money supply. It can, therefore, be used by the Fed to communicate information while not affecting current real balances. By contrast, other costly policy commitments available to the bank, such as open market operations or discount rate changes, cannot be used for purely informational purposes.

The only obvious alternative to intervention for communicating Fed information is a simple policy of announcements. But there are reasons to believe that intervention may serve an informational role in markets that cannot be served by announcements. This assumption is central to the signalling literature, in that most signalling effects could be accomplished by announcements if some liability for incorrect statements could be fully enforced. Otherwise, the Fed might find itself in a situation in which an inaccurate announcement would further one or more of its objectives. The market, anticipating this possibility, would not take announcements at their face value. In the absence of enforcement, announcements will be inferior to a policy commitment, which carries a clear and well defined set of costs.[6]

A second reason that announcements are unlikely to be useful is institutional. Announcements require extensive documentation, and careful dissemination in order to be effective, and to guard against misinterpretation. By contrast, intervention is a relatively flexible tool for alerting markets to Fed concerns. It allows the Fed to signal the arrival of new, incremental information, "remind" the market of Fed policy, or make predictions about continuously changing circumstances in a reactive, minute-by-minute manner that would be difficult with official announcements.

A third reason that intervention may be preferable to announcements is that the Fed may sometimes need to demonstrate differential information that discloses the net effects of other central banks' policies. Intervention allows the Fed to signal the exchange rate that it expects will obtain given its own future policies, as well as to signal its expectations about the policies of other central banks. The latter expectations may include information that the Fed cannot disclose directly due to existing covenants with other governments.

For a signal to be credible, there must be a cost associated with its use that is higher when the signal is false than when it is true. In the case of intervention, there are not one but several costs that the Fed bears from false signalling. The first, and perhaps most important, is loss of reputation. It is reasonable to suppose that the reputational effects of intervention policy also affect the Fed's credibility in setting domestic monetary policy (and vice versa). False signalling may also create credibility problems with other central banks. Therefore, the total reputational costs associated with false signalling can be quite large.

A second cost is direct and monetary. Intervening in the wrong direction imposes a direct financial burden on the Fed, that can be considerable when measured in terms of its total foreign currency reserves. If a central bank attempts to support a depreciating currency by signalling falsely, it purchases the currency as it declines in value. This will result in a decline in the value of the central bank's currency reserves.

B. Fed Reputation, Informative Signalling, and Targeting

In "The Case for Flexible Exchange Rates" (1953), Milton Friedman outlined two possible, and conflicting, objectives of government exchange rate intervention:

> A positive disadvantage of government speculation is the danger that government authorities operating under strong political pressures will try to peg the exchange rate, thereby converting a flexible exchange rate system into a system of rigid rates subject to change from time to time by official action... It also may be that government officials may have access to information that cannot readily be made available, for security or similar reasons, to private speculators. In any event, it would do little harm for a government agency to speculate in the exchange market provided it held to the objective of smoothing out temporary fluctuations and not interfering with fundamental adjustments. (p. 188)

This illustrates the fundamental tension underlying the signalling hypothesis. The potential conflict between what I will call the "targeting" objective of central bank policy, and the "informative" objective is particularly appropriate in analyzing foreign exchange intervention, due to the institutional authorities governing intervention decisions. If the U.S. central bank, the Fed, had autonomy in setting daily intervention policy, one might think that the desire, at the operations level of the bank, would be to engage in informative intervention. Major intervention policy initiatives, however, must be approved by, and may come directly from, the Treasury; these initiatives may override the Fed's goals and perhaps superimpose overtly political goals.[7]

The two possible government intervention objectives can be incorporated into a game, in which the foreign exchange market tries to learn whether the Fed cares about minimizing spot rate forecast errors, or targeting the spot rate.[8] In this game, when the Fed intervenes in the spot market, investors are uncertain whether it is revealing its superior information about the future path of spot rates, or whether it is simply attempting to manipulate their expectations.[9] The key feature of the game is that intervention policy aimed at minimizing the spot rate forecast error will be ineffective if the market thinks the Fed is targeting spot rates. By assuming that the market does not know the true preferences of the Fed, even if the Fed is serious about revealing useful information (ie. using intervention as an "informative" signal), the market will always expect, with positive (albeit small) probability, that the signal is false.

Consider a multi-period formulation in which intervention policy can be informative or targeting. In period t, the Fed signals by intervening in the spot market. In period t+1, information becomes available with which the market can determine the truthfulness of the period t signal. Let Δs_{t+1} denote the deviation between the post-announcement spot rate, s_{t+1}, and the current spot rate s_t.

$$\Delta s_{t+1} = s_{t+1} - s_t \tag{2}$$

Assuming that the Fed has *complete* information about the post-announcement spot rate,[10] the Fed's (truthful) signal I_t incorporates all information in Ω_{t+1}. Then substituting (1) into (2), and assuming that the market *fully* believes the Fed's signal, the spot deviation can be expressed as

$$\begin{aligned} \Delta s_{t+1} = & \frac{1}{1+\beta}\sum_{k=1}^{\infty}\left[\frac{\beta}{1+\beta}\right]^k E(z_{t+k}|\Omega_{t+1}) \\ & - \frac{1}{1+\beta}\sum_{k=0}^{\infty}\left[\frac{\beta}{1+\beta}\right]^k E(z_{t+k}|\Omega_t, I_t) = 0 \end{aligned} \tag{3}$$

To proceed, it is necessary to relax the assumption that the market fully believes the truthfulness of the Fed signal. Instead, assume that at the beginning of the game the market has some prior view about the probability that the Fed is informative, and unless this probability is high, the market will not believe the Fed's signal. So a targeting Fed has the incentive to signal truthfully, early in the game, to establish its reputation as informative; in other words, the Fed has the incentive to manipulate its reputation.[11]

The game begins with the market's initial perception of the Fed's reputation r_t, or the probability that the Fed is informative. The market then revises r_t each period using Bayes rule based on Δs_t, so that, if the Fed has signalled truthfully in previous periods, the probability that it is actually informative rises. However, the market also knows that, as the Fed's reputation increases, the probability that a targeting Fed (masquerading as informative) will target increases. As long as the Fed has complete information about the post-announcement spot rate, the Fed's reputation in period t+1 will drop to zero if the Fed signals falsely (targets) this period; while if the Fed signals truthfully, r_{t+1} is updated according to Bayes' rule:

$$\begin{aligned} r_{t+1} &= P(H|\Delta s_t=0) \\ &= \frac{P(H \text{ and } \Delta s_t=0)}{P(\Delta s_t=0)} \\ &= \frac{P(\Delta s_t=0|H)P(H)}{P(\Delta s_t=0|H)P(H) + P(\Delta s_t=0|D)P(D)} \end{aligned} \tag{4}$$

where P denotes conditional probability, H denotes honest (or informative) and D dishonest (or targeting). The second term in the denominator reflects the probability that a targeting Fed is masquerading as informative.

The Fed knows the market's updating function, and chooses its best strategy, given its current reputation and the impact that its current signalling decision will have on next period's reputation.[12] The Fed's multi-period payoff function can be written as:

$$V_f = \sum_{t=0}^{T} \beta^t[-\lambda_1(\Delta s_t)^2 + \lambda_2(\Delta s_t - \Delta s_t^e)] \tag{5}$$

where β is the Fed's discount rate; λ_1 and λ_2 are the weights that the Fed places on its informative and targeting objectives, respectively;[13] and Δs_t^e is the market's expectation of the Fed's actions, given the observed intervention signal in period t-1. Assume, for simplicity, that the Fed does not discount the future ($\beta=1$).[14]

The objective of market participants is to minimize their post-announcement forecast error, and to avoid being fooled into deviating toward a target rate.[15]

$$V_m = \sum_{t=0}^{T} \beta^t[-(\Delta s_t - \Delta s_t^e)^2] \tag{6}$$

In order to derive the Fed's optimal strategy, given that decisions are linked through time by reputational considerations,[16] begin by examining the Fed's incentives in the final period. Denote the probabilities that both the Fed and the market play zero (the Fed signals truthfully and the market believes the signal) in a mixed strategy as m_t and f_t for the market and the Fed respectively. The expected return for a targeting Fed in the last period is derived over each of four possible payoffs:[17]

$$\begin{aligned} V_f^e(r_T) &= m_T\left[f_T(0) + (1-f_T)\left(\frac{\lambda_2^2}{4\lambda_1}\right)\right] \\ &+ (1-m_T)\left[f_T\left(\frac{-\lambda_2^2}{2\lambda_1}\right) + (1-f_T)\left(\frac{-\lambda_2^2}{4\lambda_1}\right)\right] \\ &= \frac{\lambda_2^2}{4\lambda_1}[2m_T - 1 - f_T] \end{aligned} \tag{7}$$

The Fed's expected payoff function V_f^e is defined as a linear function of f_T. Hence, as long as V_f^e is decreasing in f_T, it will not pay an uncommitted Fed to play zero in the final period. Likewise, the market's expected return over the four possible payoffs is derived (using (5) and (6))[18] as:

$$
\begin{aligned}
V_m^e(r_T) &= m_T\left[r_T(0) + (1-r_T)\left(\frac{-\lambda_2^2}{4\lambda_1^2}\right)\right] \\
&\quad + (1-m_T)\left[r_T\left(\frac{-\lambda_2^2}{4\lambda_1^2}\right) + (1-r_T)(0)\right] \qquad (8) \\
&= \frac{\lambda_2^2}{4\lambda_1^2}[m_T(2r_t - 1) - r_T]
\end{aligned}
$$

This result implies that if the Fed's reputation is high in the last period ($r_T > 1/2$) the market will always play $m_T = 1$ ($\Delta s_T^e = 0$). On the other hand, if $r_T < 1/2$, it will not pay the market to believe the Fed signal, so that it will always play $m_T = 0$ ($\Delta s_T^e = \lambda_2/2\lambda_1$). Finally, if $r_T = 1/2$ the market will be indifferent about m_T ($m_T = 1/2$). The equilibrium strategy in this case ($m_T = 1/2$ when $r_T = 1/2$) is assumed to depend on the equilibrium conditions in the preceding period.

The key is that, in order for a targeting Fed to build its reputation (so that $r_T > 1/2$), it must play $f_t = 1$ for $t = 1, \ldots, T-1$ (where T is the period in which the Fed plans to "surprise" the market by signalling falsely (targeting)). This strategy, however, also involves the risk that the market will play $m_t = 0$ during the Fed's reputation building period, because the market realizes the incentives of a masquerading Fed. Recall that the one-period cost of $\Delta s_t = 0$ and $\Delta s_t^e = \lambda_2/2\lambda_1$ to the Fed is $-\lambda_2^2/2\lambda_1$; it is the worst outcome of the four possible payoffs.[19] Further, period T can be interpreted as final in the sense that, as soon as the Fed targets, its reputation as informative falls to zero and the game is ended.

While the resolution of this game illustrates the Fed's dual objectives, and the market's ability to deter the Fed from conveying false signals, the deterrence in some sense is too strong, and the equilibrium is too stable. If, however, we allow for the fact that the Fed has only *incomplete* information about the post-announcement spot rate (i.e. $\Omega_t + I_t \neq \Omega_{t+1}$), so that $\Delta s_t \neq 0$ even when the Fed has signalled informatively, then it is no longer strictly rational for investors to set $r_{t+1} = 0$ if $\Delta s_t \neq 0$.[20] Such a case is not explicitly treated in the above model. However, if period t's unanticipated (confounding) news is a white noise process, then $\Sigma \Delta s_t$ should tend to zero over time, and investors can, therefore, determine on average if the Fed is informative.[21] If this is the case, the spot price in the beginning of a low reputation period may reflect a positive, but declining, probability that the Fed is informative. Likewise, the Fed's reputation may increase more gradually than in the perfect information case during periods in which the Fed is indeed informative.

III. IMPLEMENTING SIGNALLING TESTS: DISTINGUISHING FED REPUTATION

Within the signalling hypothesis, intervention's influence on the exchange rate depends critically on the central bank's reputation for sending truthful signals. Even fully informative intervention may have no effect (or the opposite of its intended effect) on exchange rates, if Fed credibility is low. Moreover, if the market's perception of Fed credibility changes over time, the effectiveness of any given amount of intervention is also likely to change. Consequently, conditioning on the basis of changes in Fed credibility is critical to implementing tests of whether (and when) sterilized intervention can influence spot rates.

It is difficult to specify a fully satisfactory technique for estimating Fed credibility. Any attempt to construct a direct estimate of r_t as defined in Section II's model, through the specification of a lag structure on informativeness across previous periods, inevitably imposes an arbitrary specification on both the horizon used by the market to estimate reputation, and the way that reputation increases and dissipates. In this section I present two alternative approaches to the problem of identifying when a central bank is viewed as credible by the market. Both approaches are implemented empirically in the next section.

A. A Sampling Procedure

One way to condition on central bank credibility is to isolate subperiods in the sample when r_t is most likely to be high initially. Central banks periodically announce major shifts in monetary policy. Presumably, the purpose of these announcements is to influence the public's perception of the central bank's commitment to its stated objectives. These announced policy shifts can, therefore, be used to identify periods when the central bank's reputation is high (at least initially).

A major policy shift was defined as a contemporaneous change in at least two of the main instruments of monetary policy--i.e. a change in the money supply (or interest rate) target and the discount rate--and the "package" of changes had to be announced as a major new initiative by the Fed. *Ex post*, it turns out that these sampling criteria are very strict. In the 1977-1981 period examined, only two such major policy changes were announced by the Fed. One marked the Carter-Miller "anti-inflation" package on November 1, 1978; and the other began the shift in Fed policy to M1 targeting instituted by Volcker on October 6, 1979.

To determine the enddates for each "high-reputation" subperiod, all Fed statements containing information about future monetary policy[22], and covered in the *Wall Street Journal Index*, were isolated. Statements about intervention per se were excluded, so as not to bias the intervention tests by selecting subperiods based on the effectiveness of intervention. Exchange rate reactions were used to measure the credibility of each statement, based on the assumption that a major pronouncement by the central bank is likely to constitute the central determinant of exchange rate reactions on announcement days.[23] For each statement or "event-day," an expected exchange rate reaction was determined conditional on the Fed being believed. Then, the actual one-day rate change accompanying the announcement was calculated, and compared to the expected change. If the sign matched, this was viewed as a credible statement, while if the sign was the opposite of that expected, the statement was not viewed as credible. The end of each high-reputation subperiod was defined to occur when Fed statements were disbelieved for two straight months.

Table 2.1 presents a summary of the subperiod dates as isolated using this sampling procedure, as well as the proportion of believed statements in each subperiod. The statistics show significant divergence in the high-and low-credibility subperiods, based on the proportion of believed and disbelieved statements. Appendix B lists the announcements that were used for the tests.

The sampling procedure isolates two subperiods, covering, in total, approximately one of the four years under examination,[24] during which the Fed was most likely perceived as honest and informative by the market. These comprise periods in which intervention, if it is to have a signalling effect, should have been believed. While it is possible that these subperiods are needlessly restrictive, they allow an "upper bound" test for the informativeness of intervention. If intervention does not appear to have significant signalling effects during these two subperiods, it is unclear when it could be used effectively for this purpose by the Fed.

B. Time-Varying Parameter Estimation

A second approach to identifying periods in which the Fed's reputation is high explicitly incorporates estimates of the changing motives and credibility of the Fed. Time-varying parameter estimation techniques are used to allow regression coefficient values to change both discretely and gradually over time.

A number of test procedures have been developed to test for discrete parameter shifts when the timing of the policy shift is unknown. The test used here, the cusum square test, is based on a statistic that is computed as the ratio of the squared recursive residual[25], up to time t, to the squared recursive residual for the full period (Brown, Durbin and Evans (1975)). Intuitively, if a regression relationship shifts at time t, the forecast for period t based on estimates calculated from the first t-1 observations should be less accurate than analogous forecasts for the periods prior to the shift date. The significance bands for the cusum square statistic, under the null hypothesis of no shift in the regression, are presented in Table 1 of Durbin (1969).

The cusum square test provides evidence on whether there are sharp changes in regression parameter values over time. Its limitation is a potential lack of power. Therefore, where the test yields evidence that parameter values shift significantly, I then complement this test with a Chow (1960) test centered on the apparent shift date.

Once shift dates have been identified in time-series regressions, there remains an additional unresolved issue in specifying the Fed's behavior and credibility in the periods surrounding these significant shifts. For example, an identifiable change in Fed credibility does not imply that credibility was stable either before or after the apparent regime change. Rather, it is likely that Fed credibility changes both discretely and gradually over time. Blanchard (1984) suggests that evidence from the financial press supports the hypothesis that Volcker's October 1979 change to M1-targeting was perceived as a regime shift--but that the shift was not fully believed by the market until the first half of 1981.

Consequently, a final part of the test methodology examines whether, in the subperiods prior to and after significant shift-dates, regression parameter values are stable. These test statistics are based on the Watson (1980) LM test for time-varying regression coefficients. The null hypothesis is that the regression coefficients are constant, and the alternative is that the parameters vary over time according to a first-order autoregressive process.[26]

Where the null hypothesis of parameter stability is rejected, estimates of the regression parameter values are tested for time variation. The test for time-varying coefficients involves regressing the parameter of interest, for example δ_1, on a constant and its lagged value.

$$\delta_{1t} = \gamma_0 + \gamma_1 \delta_{1t-1} + \varepsilon_t \tag{9}$$

This specification is general in the sense that it encompasses both the random-walk model ($\gamma_1 = 1$) and the random coefficients model ($\gamma_1 = 0$). Maximum likelihood solutions to the time-varying parameter (TVP) system are found using a Kalman filtering program.[27]

This test methodology, taken in sum, allows the tests to explicitly incorporate varying Fed behavior and credibility. The tests determine on an *ex ante* basis whether sharp shifts occur in the regression relationships, and whether these relationships are stable over time between shift dates.

IV. THE INFORMATIVENESS OF INTERVENTION: A DIRECT TEST

A first set of tests of the signalling hypothesis examines directly whether intervention is related to *inside* Fed information about the money supply and its own policy response. Part A of this section describes the intervention data used for the empirical tests. Part B describes the test of intervention's informativeness.

A. Data Description

The tests presented in this chapter were facilitated by a unique opportunity to work with the combined Bundesbank and Fed daily intervention data for the dollar/deutschemark market, spanning the period January 1977 through March 1985. The intervention data series measure intervention by the U.S. and German central banks, in dollars, at current market values. The data provided by the Bundesbank separates EMS intervention, which is not at the discretion of the Bundesbank, but depends on official EMS realignment agreements, from discretionary Bundesbank intervention. Only non-EMS, discretionary intervention was used in the following tests.

The U.S. data include both "passive" and "active" intervention. Passive intervention, or customer transactions, include Fed purchases and sales of foreign currency with customers who would otherwise have dealt with market agents.[28] It is important to recognize that, since the timing of so-called "passive" intervention is under the discretion of the Fed, its potential to serve as a signal is not impaired. Therefore, in aggregating the U.S. data, no distinction between the two was made.

B. Intervention and Money Announcements

There are two potential motives for intervention policy within the signalling hypothesis. Intervention may serve to communicate *inside* information about future monetary policy, or intervention may be undertaken to mislead the market, and hence be effectively disassociated from underlying monetary policy. These two motives can be distinguished empirically by combining intervention data with available data reflecting market expectations of monetary policy. These data allow us to examine whether, and when, intervention conveys information about *unanticipated* monetary policy. The assumption is that, if intervention constitutes a signal, it should provide information to the market when there is a difference between the central bank's *inside* information and the market's current expectations.

Unexpected future money is proxied in the empirical work with the U.S. weekly money surprise, calculated as the difference between the M1 stock number that is announced each Thursday,[29] and the market's expectation of that announcement as reported by survey on the previous Tuesday.[30] The M1 data announced each Thursday are for the fiscal week that ended nine days earlier, on the previous Wednesday. The monetary base and its components are announced a week earlier, so the Thursday announcement releases information about the previous week's bank multiplier, rather than about discretionary actions by the Fed. The surprise, or the unanticipated component of (last week's) money supply, however, may convey important news to the market about *future* Fed policy.

Previous studies have shown that, on average in the post-October 1979 period, news of a positive money surprise was associated with a subsequent rise in short term interest rates and appreciation of the dollar against other currencies. One explanation for the appreciation of the dollar is that the market anticipated offsetting future monetary policy in response to positive surprises. A positive money surprise, therefore, may have been a leading indicator of future monetary contraction in the post-October 1979 period. In contrast, during the pre-October 1979 period, a positive money surprise on average resulted in higher short-term interest rates and dollar depreciation, implying that the market did not anticipate offsetting Fed policy.[31]

If the Fed knows *ex ante* that the money supply is larger than the market's expectation, and the Fed intends to offset the money-surprise in the future with contractionary policy, then the Fed can convey this information to the market using dollar supporting intervention policy. In this case, the actual money supply announcement, and its consequence for future Fed policy, can be thought of as old information because it will have already been conveyed through intervention policy.[32]

We can test whether intervention is related to unexpected future money by regressing intervention on the money surprise.

$$I_{t,2} = \delta_0 + \delta_1 (m^a_{t+2} - m^e_t) + v_{t,2} \qquad H_0 : \delta_1 = 0 \qquad (10)$$

Money supply surprises (m^a_{t+2} - m^e_t) were derived by subtracting weekly MMS predictions[33] (taken on Tuesdays) from the actual (first published) money supply announcement on Thursdays (or Fridays). The dependent variable, interim U.S. intervention ($I_{t,2}$), was accumulated between the Tuesday expectation and the Thursday announcement (or Friday, when appropriate). In the regression, the coefficient on the money surprise variable should be significantly different from zero in those periods when the Fed is intervening to inform the market of the future monetary policy implications of the surprise between Tuesday and Thursday. In periods when the Fed is engaged in targeting policy, no relationship should be observed between the money surprise and preceding intervention.

Table 2.2 presents estimates of equation (10) for the five subperiods isolated using the sample procedure described in the previous section. The regression results are supportive of the hypothesis that the Fed uses intervention to leak future announcement information during high-reputation subperiods. The coefficient on the money surprise variable, δ_1, is significant at the 5% level in both high-reputation subperiods. In the low-reputation subperiods, the relationship is not significant. This indicates a different motive for intervention in the low-reputation periods, showing it to be unconnected to this important *inside* information. It is interesting to note that ρ (the serial correlation coefficient) is highly significant in the three low-reputation subperiods. This implies that past intervention explains a substantial portion of current intervention in low-reputation subperiods.

The first step in implementing the time-varying parameter approach is to estimate equation (10) over the full sample period (1977-1981), and use the cusum square test to check for parameter stability. Figure 2.1 presents a plot of the cusum square statistic from the regression over the full sample period. A deviation of the cusum squares plot of .112 or greater from the 45-degree line allows rejection of the null hypothesis of stable coefficients at the .10 level.[34] The cusum square statistic exceeds the critical bands in late 1978, Fall 1979, and Spring 1980. Thus, the test indicates that, in these three periods, the relationship between money surprises and intervention changed significantly.

The first two periods indicated by the cusum plot coincide roughly with the two major announced monetary regime changes by the Fed isolated in the sampling procedure presented in Section III: the Carter-Miller Anti-Inflation Package announced on November 1, 1978 and the Volcker shift to M1-targeting announced on October 6, 1979. The third period coincides with the Carter-Volcker Special Credit Control Program announced on March 14, 1980. Table 2.3 presents the results of Chow and Forecast[35] tests for a shift in equation (10) after the three potential shift dates. The pre- and post-shift-date subsamples for the Chow tests contain thirty (weekly) observations before the potential shift date, and thirty after the date. Both of these tests corroborate the presence of discrete changes in parameter values at the first two but not the third potential shift date.[36]

I next examine whether, *within* the three subperiods, the parameter values of the regression vary significantly over time, using the Watson LM test. The Watson test results presented in Table 2.3 provide strong evidence that the slope coefficient does vary significantly over time during the first and second but not the third subperiod. (For the post-Credit Control Program period the constant term shows evidence of time variation at the 0.07 level.) Thus, the test implies that the time-varying coefficient estimation technique is warranted by the data in the first two subperiods.

Table 2.4 presents fixed-parameter and time-varying parameter estimates of equation (10), for the two subperiods isolated by the cusum square and Chow tests. The fixed coefficient estimates allow both for serial correlation and heteroskedasticity in the errors.[37] These parameter estimates, presented in the top half of Table 2.4, do not provide support for the hypothesis that the Fed uses intervention to leak information about future monetary policy. The coefficient on the money surprise variable is insignificant in both subperiods. However, the serial correlation coefficient, ρ, is highly significant and positive, suggesting that past intervention explains a substantial portion of current intervention in both subperiods. These fixed parameter estimates are analogous to those presented in Table 2.2, only in this case subperiods two and three are combined, and periods four and five are combined.

The estimates allowing for time variation in the slope coefficient, presented in the lower half of Table 2.4, provide evidence in favor of the signalling hypothesis. The relationship between money surprises and intervention is statistically significant in the subperiod following the Carter-Miller Anti-Inflation Package announcement, and in the post-October 1979 period. While the fit of the time-varying parameter model is better (in terms of error variances), than that of the fixed parameter model for both subperiods, the size and sign of both the constant and the coefficient of first-order serial correlation are similar under both estimation techniques.

For both subperiods, the mean time-varying slope coefficient estimate, denoted as $\bar{\delta}_{1t}$, is significant at the .01 level. While in the M1-targeting period the mean value of the time-varying slope parameter is slightly smaller than the fixed estimate, in the Carter-Miller subperiod it is roughly 10 times larger than the corresponding fixed parameter estimate. The estimate of γ_1 is close to unity for the Carter-Miller period, suggesting that the δ_{1t} process in the months following the announcement of the Anti-Inflation Package resembles a random walk.

Figures 2.2 and 2.3 graph the estimated δ_{1t}'s for the Carter-Miller and the post October 1979 periods, respectively, over time. Figure 2.2 shows that the relationship between money surprises and intervention was highly unstable during the Carter-Miller period. Although the TVP slope estimate is significantly positive, little can be said concerning the informativeness of Fed intervention. In contrast, Figure 2.3 shows a positive relationship between money surprises and intervention in the post-October 1979 period. The dramatic dip in the parameter plot coincides roughly with the announcement of the Carter-Volcker Special

Credit Control Program.

The evidence from Figure 2.3 suggests that intervention was informative in the immediate aftermath of Volcker's announced shift to M1-targeting. During this period, there was a significant positive relationship between intervention and money surprises. It is particularly significant that this period is the one most strongly supporting the signalling hypothesis. The macroeconomic literature generally characterizes this period as one in which the Fed's anti-inflation stance was perceived as credible (Huizinga and Mishkin (1986)). The stated anti-inflationary goals of the Fed were, in fact, backed by policy and believed by the market. Thus, the evidence, in showing that intervention was informative in this period, corroborates other evidence on the credibility of Fed monetary policy.

The time-series behavior of the regression coefficients is also revealing. In the wake of Volcker's switch to M1-targeting, the relationship between intervention and money surprises builds and falls off in two five to six month cycles. This pattern is consistent with an intuitive notion of a reputation-building process in a world with imperfect information. A discrete policy shift ushers in a period in which the market is ready to believe current signals with more certainty. Reputation builds as long as past signals continue to prove correct.

V. INTERVENTION, SIGNALLING, AND EXCHANGE RATES

In this section, two tests for a relationship between intervention and the path of exchange rates are developed. Intervention policy and exchange rate movements may be simultaneously determined. If exchange rates enter central banks' objective functions, then monetary policy and hence informative intervention signals, will be influenced by exchange rate movements. Central banks may also intervene in a manner inconsistent with future monetary policy intentions in order to explicitly manipulate exchange rate expectations. Under either scenario, contemporaneous movements in exchange rates may influence central bank decisions to intervene; consequently, intervention can not be assumed to be exogenous.

A. An Upper Bound to the Exchange Rate Effects of Intervention

A simple approach to testing the maximum observed effect of intervention on spot rates involves isolating the largest intervention events in the daily time series, and determining their average effect on intervention-day spot rate changes. Conditioning on a few, relatively large, intervention decisions, and examining their short-term impacts, is likely to minimize the problem of confounding information and possible simultaneity. This strategy minimizes the window over which changes are measured, and conditions on events that are most likely to show central tendencies of the exchange rate process.

To isolate the largest daily intervention events, the time series of U.S. intervention from January 1977 through February 1981 was sampled for all days whose daily dollar intervention exceeded $300 million. Confidentiality agreements prevent the presentation of a full frequency distribution of the daily intervention series, and, therefore, prevent a full description of the relationship of these events to the daily time series. The sampling approach yielded thirty-five observations (19 in the high-reputation subperiods and 16 in the low-reputation subperiods defined in the Table 2.1), placing them within the .05 tail of the distribution. Further, the tail of the distribution is thin; that is, there are many zero and small (e.g., less than $100 million) intervention days.

Only positive intervention days (that is, dollar-supporting days) were isolated. While it would also be useful to examine the average effects of large negative (dollar sales) days, the 1977-1981 period did not yield a sufficient number of significantly large negative intervention days to facilitate useful tests.

Due to the relatively short length of the time series involved, several of the major intervention events are closely bunched in time. This precludes a full event-study approach to examining the significance of the average spot price reaction to the intervention events, since preceding events confound the variance of a pre-event portfolio of exchange rate changes. Therefore, the approach taken was cross-sectional. Spot changes on large intervention event dates were grouped, and a cross-sectional average was examined for statistical significance. For comparison purposes, a random sample of 100 daily spot changes was drawn from the full time series of spot changes (1977-1981), to examine the variance and average change in a control case.

Table 2.5 presents the resulting summary statistics for the high-reputation intervention events, the low-credibility events, and the control sample. Included are statistics for the mean one-day rate change, the t-statistic of the mean estimate, and the nonparametric distribution of changes between positive and negative. The changes are calculated as $[(s_{t+1}/s_t)-1]$ where s_t is defined as dollar/mark. As can be seen, the results show quite striking support for the signalling hypothesis, despite the small sample size. In the control sample, the mean one-day change is very small, at .0003, and insignificant. The high-reputation signalling events, by contrast, are associated with a one-day mean positive spot change of -.004, nearly a full order of magnitude larger. The t-statistic, despite the small sample size, is -3.7. Finally, the low-reputation intervention events are associated with a .0009 spot change, a change that is of the wrong sign given the direction of the intervention events, and is also insignificant. The relative frequency of positive and negative daily changes in the three samples also show a strong and consistent divergence.

These results suggest that at its upper bound, in periods when the Fed is credible, intervention has a significant average effect on spot rates. The economic significance of the average effect, at .4%, is a matter for conjecture. The difference in market reaction between the high- and low-reputation subperiods offers support for the joint hypothesis that credibility matters, and that the reputation-based subperiods isolated in this chapter are meaningful.

B. Intervention and the Forward Rate

There is an approach to estimating the time-series influence of intervention on exchange rates that avoids the potential simultaneity problem. This approach examines whether today's observed intervention helps explain the predictable component of ex post excess returns in the foreign exchange market.[38] Ex post excess returns are defined as the realized profit a trader would make simultaneously borrowing in one currency and lending in another. Over the period t to t+k, the ex post excess return, $e_{t,k}$, is calculated as:

$$e_{t,k} = (1 + i_{t,k}) - (1 + i^*_{t,k})\left(\frac{s_{t+k}}{s_t}\right) \tag{11}$$

If we rearrange equation (11) and substitute in the forward exchange rate, $f_{t,k}$, then the ex post excess return is expressed as

$$e_{t,k} = (f_{t,k} - s_{t+k})\left(\frac{1+i^*_{t,k}}{s_t}\right) \tag{12}$$

The forward rate can be further decomposed into the expected spot exchange rate and the expected risk premium ($f_{t,k} = s^e_{t+k} + rp^e_{t,k}$). A regression of ex post excess returns on variables observed at time t or earlier provides a test of the joint hypothesis that the expected risk premium is zero and that the spot exchange market is informationally efficient.[39]

$$e_{t,k} = \beta_0 + \beta_1 x_t + \eta_{t,k} \qquad H_0{:}\beta_1 = 0 \tag{13}$$

If it is assumed that expectations are rational ($s_{t+k} - s^e_{t+k} = \xi_{t+k}$ where ξ_{t+k} is a white noise prediction error), then the regression coefficient β_1 in equation (13) reduces to $cov(rp^e_{t,k}, x_t)/var(x_t)$. If x_t includes intervention, then (13) allows a direct test of intervention's influence on the expected risk premium. However, if one allows for systematic prediction errors, (evidence in support of which was presented in Chapter 1), β_1 will reflect the covariance of both expected depreciation and any risk premium with intervention.

Equation (13) is estimated using annualized weekly observations of the one-month-ahead dollar/mark ex post excess return, $e_{t,4}$.[40] The relevant institutional features of forward contract delivery timing are taken into account, as discussed in detail by Meese and Singleton (1982). Because the data is overlapping, OLS estimation will be biased; the disturbances are no longer guaranteed to be serially uncorrelated. In order to take into account the moving average structure of the disturbances, the regressions were estimated using Hansen's (1982) heteroskedasticity and autocorrelation consistent asymptotic covariance matrix, assuming a moving average process of order 3 (k-1 where k=4 weeks).

The specification of (13) that was estimated is:

$$e_{t,k} = \beta_o + \beta_1 I^{US}_{1,t-2} + \beta_2 I^{WG}_{1,t-2} + \eta_{t,k} \tag{14}$$

The independent variables, denoted $I^{US}_{1,t-2}$ and $I^{WG}_{1,t-2}$ are U.S. and West

German intervention accumulated from the beginning of the sample (t=1) through period t-2. Spot foreign exchange contracts for marks must be ordered two days before delivery, and market convention requires that currency transactions be made prior to investment transactions. This convention, therefore, requires the right-hand-side variables in equation (14) to be known in period t-2 or earlier. Intervention enters cumulatively in the regressions, to reflect changes in current relative outside supplies of foreign and domestic assets. If there exist risk premia on dollar assets that are increasing functions of the current and future relative supply of dollar assets held by the public, then intervention (defined as net purchases of dollar assets) should be negatively correlated with ex post excess dollar returns. A sterilized sale of dollar assets that signals future expansionary Fed monetary policy should, for example,lead to an increase in the expected dollar risk premia. Investors will require a higher return on dollar assets in order to willingly hold the larger current and future outstanding stock of dollar assets.

Equation (14) is estimated over the high- and low-reputation subperiods isolated in Section III. Time-varying parameter techniques could not be used because of the overlapping data problem. Further, the small sample of weekly data precluded estimation of the short-lived Carter-Miller regime. Therefore, subperiods two and three, listed in Table 2.1, were combined into one subperiod.

Table 2.6 presents ex post excess return regression results over four subperiods and over the full sample. The coefficient on U.S. intervention enters significantly in three of the four subperiods, but with the wrong (positive) sign in the first low-reputation subperiod. A significant negative β_1 implies that Fed purchases of dollars were associated with higher expected dollar appreciation, and/or larger mark risk premia. An one-million-dollar intervention purchase by the Fed over the Volcker regime (subperiod three) decreased the annualized one-month dollar-mark differential by 64 basis points. The coefficient on West German intervention enters significantly in all but the first subperiod, but always with the wrong sign. A significant positive β_2 implies that Bundesbank purchases of dollars increased the dollar risk premium. Over the full sample, neither U.S. nor West German intervention had a statistically significant influence on ex post excess returns.

Overall, the regression results presented in Table 2.6 indicate that both Fed and Bundesbank intervention operations influenced market expectations in some periods. After November 1978 the market generally bet with the Fed, but bet against the Bundesbank. One explanation for this pattern is that the subperiods were selected on the basis of Fed, and not Bundesbank, reputation. These results are consistent with the joint hypothesis that the Fed uses intervention as a signalling device, and that the signals can effectively influence market expectations in periods when the Fed's reputation for honesty is high.

VI. SUMMARY AND CONCLUSIONS

This chapter proposes that Fed intervention in foreign exchange markets may be motivated by its ability to signal new information that is otherwise difficult to make public to market participants; this information then influences exchange rate expectations. Intervention has significant advantages over other possible methods of communicating information, including flexibility, timeliness, and the ability to maintain secrecy agreements with other central banks. Intervention carries the characteristic typical of credible financial signals, specifically, that costs are differentially higher with false than with true signals.

The chapter presents a set of empirical tests of the signalling hypothesis, in which a distinction was made between subperiods where the Fed appeared credible and periods in which it appeared non-credible. Tests utilize daily intervention data, over the period 1977 through 1981, from the U.S. Federal Reserve and the German Bundesbank, both provided by confidential agreement.[41]

A first set of tests examines directly whether intervention contains information about the future course of Fed monetary policy. The tests examine whether a relationship existed between intervention and weekly money surprises, using publicly available pre-announcement money supply forecasts. A primary role of intervention, if it acts as a signal, is to leak information about future Fed policy conditional on the emerging behavior of the money stock. The tests confirm that, in high-reputation subperiods, intervention carries significant information about the policy implications of future money supply behavior.

A second set of tests examines the effect of intervention on exchange rate formation during high- and low-credibility periods. Overall, these tests tend to support the signalling hypothesis. Evidence indicates that on days when the Fed intervenes heavily, and has high credibility, the average exchange rate reaction is significantly biased in the direction implied by the intervention. Indeed, the average exchange rate reaction to large interventions appears a full order of magnitude larger than the average daily exchange rate change over a random sample, although the economic significance of the intervention-caused change remains open to debate. A regression of ex post excess returns on U.S. and West German intervention corroborates this result. Interventions against the dollar, by the Fed, led to an increase in ex post dollar excess returns. This suggests that investors required an higher return on dollar assets in order to willingly hold the larger current and future outstanding stock of dollar assets.

Taken together, these results provide suggestive support for the signalling hypothesis. They show that, in periods when the market believes that the Fed is being truthful, intervention releases information to the market, and exchange rates react accordingly.

TABLE 2.1

Credibility Subperiods

Beginning and end dates of credibility subperiods, and frequency of believed Fed statements in each subperiod. Fed statements were defined as believed if the associated actual exchange rate reaction corresponded with the expected reaction conditional on the statement being believed. Statements included all major Fed announcements carried in the *Wall Street Journal Index* during the measurement period, excluding statements directly about intervention policy and money supply announcements.

Subperiod Dates	Frequency of Believed Fed Statements	Fed Reputation
1/77 - 10/78	.38	Low
11/78 - 5/79	.93	High
5/79 - 10/79	.15	Low
10/79 - 3/80	.87	High
4/80 - 2/81	.43	Low
Full Sample	.51	
Pre-October 1979	.44	
Post-October 1979	.58	

TABLE 2.2

Money Surprises and Fed Intervention

Relationship between money surprise and intervention during the interim period. $I_{t,2}$ denotes intervention (x10^{-3}); m^a_{t+2} denotes ultimate money announcement, and m^e_t denotes Tuesday money expectation.

$$I_{t,2} = \delta_0 + \delta_1(m^a_{t+2} - m^e_t) + v_{t,2}$$

Regressions were estimated assuming first-order serially correlated errors (corrected using Cochrane-Orcutt). ρ is the coefficient of the first-order autoregressive structural error process; the R^2 and other summary statistics are based upon the complete model where $v_t = \rho v_{t-1} + \epsilon_t$, and, therefore, use ϵ's rather than v's. * denotes rejection at the .05 level and ** at the .01 level for the hypotheses that the coefficient equals zero. Reputational subperiods (r) are denoted as (H) high-reputation and (L) low-reputation.

Subperiod	r	δ_0	δ_1	ρ	R^2	DW	SEE
9/77 - 10/78	L	0.097	-0.016	0.701	.31	1.68	.174
		(1.09)	(-1.184)	(4.359)**			
11/78 - 4/79	H	0.062	0.132	0.214	.19	2.06	.361
		(0.489)	(2.145)*	(0.932)			
5/79 - 10/79	L	0.251	-0.063	0.426	.20	1.70	.395
		(1.707)	(-1.088)	(2.110)*			
10/79 - 3/80	H	-0.158	0.047	0.349	.26	2.07	.287
		(-1.790)	(2.020)*	(1.725)			
4/80 - 2/81	L	-0.146	-0.004	0.596	.45	1.95	.194
		(-2.017)*	(-0.430)	(5.938)**			
9/77 - 2/81		-0.005	0.006	0.494	.24	2.04	.292
full sample		(-0.117)	(0.567)	(7.488)**			

TABLE 2.3

Tests For Discrete and Continuous Parameter Variability

Preliminary Diagnostics on equation (10):

$$I_{t,2} = \delta_0 + \delta_1(m^a_{t+2} - m^e_t) + v_{t,2}$$

to test for discrete and continuous time-varying parameter values. $I_{t,2}$ denotes intervention ($x10^{-3}$); m^a_{t+2} denotes ultimate money announcement, and m^e_t denotes Tuesday money expectation.

Potential shift dates include the Carter-Miller Anti-Inflation Package announced on November 1, 1978, Volcker's change to M1-targeting announced on October 6, 1979, and the Carter-Volcker Special Credit Control Program announced on March 14, 1980. Available sample is 9/77-2/81 (177 weekly observations).

Shift-Date	Chow test[a]		Forecast test[b]		Watson Test[c]	
	F-stat	P[d]	F-stat	P	coeff.	P
Nov. 1, 1978	7.05	1.000	5.58	1.000	δ_0	0.698
					δ_1	0.999
Oct. 6, 1979	3.13	0.966	1.57	0.980	δ_0	0.780
					δ_1	0.961
Mar. 14, 1980	0.80	0.504	0.79	0.138	δ_0	0.933
					δ_1	0.534

a) The F-statistic for the Chow tests is distributed as F(3,54).

b) The F-statistic for the Forecast Tests is distributed across the three shift dates as F(50,103), F(50,151) and F(50,173) respectively.

c) The Watson LM Test for the presence of an autoregressive transition parameter is based on a statistical approximation using a grid search of 0.05 width.

d) P is the probability of rejection of the null hypothesis of no discrete (or continuous) change in the parameter value.

TABLE 2.4
Money Surprises and Fed Intervention

Relationship between money surprise and intervention during the interim period. $I_{t,2}$ denotes intervention (x10^{-3}); m^a_{t+2} denotes ultimate money announcement, and m^e_t denotes Tuesday money expectation.

$$I_{t,2} = \delta_0 + \delta_1(m^a_{t+2} - m^e_t) + v_{t,2}$$

Regressions were estimated assuming first-order serially correlated errors (corrected using Cochrane-Orcutt). ρ is the coefficient of the first-order autoregressive structural error process. $\bar{\delta}_{1t}$ is the mean value of the time-varying-parameter δ_{1t}. * denotes rejection at the .05 level and ** at the .01 level of the hypothesis that the coefficient equals zero.

Fixed Coefficient Estimates

Carter-Miller regime Sample: 10/24/78 to 8/28/79	Coeff.	Std.Err.	Volcker regime Sample: 9/25/79 to 2/17/81	Coeff.	Std.Err.
δ_0	0.0822	0.1370	δ_0	-0.1085	0.1018
δ_1	0.0032	0.0429	δ_1	0.0115	0.0106
ρ	0.3556	0.1438**	ρ	0.4362	0.0931**
σ^2_v	0.1698		σ^2_v	0.0747	
R^2	0.127		R^2	0.234	
D.W.	1.895		D.W.	2.056	

Maximum Likelihood Time Varying Coefficient Estimates
transition equation: $\delta_{1t} = \gamma_0 + \gamma_1\delta_{1t-1} + \varepsilon_t$

δ_0	0.1011	0.0992	δ_0	-0.1197	0.0586*
ρ	0.3289	0.1500**	ρ	0.4323	0.0926**
γ_0	0.0017	0.0098	γ_0	0.0019	0.0041
γ_1	0.9456	0.3394**	γ_1	0.7066	0.4851
$\bar{\delta}_{1t}$	0.0377	0.0125**	$\bar{\delta}_{1t}$	0.0078	0.0005**
σ^2_v	0.1674	0.0393**	σ^2_v	0.0718	0.0124**
σ^2_ε	0.00001	0.0000*	σ^2_ε	0.0000	0.0000*

TABLE 2.5

Spot Reactions to Large Intervention Events

Mean percentage change in the $/DM spot rate, measured in the one-day interval surrounding major daily U.S. intervention events (observations are for 9AM EST). All intervention events are dollar-supporting, and occurred during the period January 1977-February 1981. Samples are nineteen events occurring in high-reputation subperiods; and sixteen events in low-reputation subperiods. Compared to a control sample of 100 daily changes drawn at random from the period January 1977-February 1981.

sample	$\Delta\overline{s}$ (t-stat)	% pos	% neg
High-reputation intervention (n=19)	-.00415 (-3.71)	.90	.10
Low-reputation intervention (n=16)	.00090 (0.88)	.19	.81
Control spot changes (100 random)	.00030 (0.64)	.47	.53

TABLE 2.6
Intervention Effects on Ex Post Excess Returns

The effect of U.S. and German intervention on weekly changes in one-month-ahead ex post excess returns

$$e_{t,k} = \beta_o + \beta_1 I_{1,t-2}^{US} + \beta_2 I_{1,t-2}^{WG} + \eta_{t,k}$$

Ex post \$/DM excess returns are observed weekly and annualized. Intervention variables are in dollars, multiplied by 10^{-4}, and accumulated from the beginning of the sample, 1/1/77. $\eta_{t,k}$ are assumed to follow a 4-week moving-average process. Numbers in parentheses are the estimated t-statistics for corrected standard errors. * denotes rejection at the .05 level and ** at the .01 level for the hypotheses that the coefficient equals zero. Reputational subperiods (r) are denoted as (H) high-reputation and (L) low-reputation.

Subperiod	r	β_0	β_1	β_2	R^2	SEE	OBS
1/77 - 10/78	L	-0.027	1.937	-0.422	.01	.279	92
		(-0.370)	(2.149)*	(-1.389)			
11/78 - 10/79	H	-2.559	-0.217	2.896	.08	.229	49
		(-3.090)**	(-1.289)	(3.182)**			
11/79 - 3/80	H	0.166	-6.448	4.786	.11	.225	23
		(0.272)	(-3.978)**	(2.706)**			
4/80 - 12/81	L	-0.109	-0.714	0.787	.06	.391	94
		(-0.707)	(-1.962)*	(1.958)*			
1/77 - 12/81		-0.069	-0.164	0.243	.03	.365	258
full sample		(-0.898)	(-0.586)	(1.073)			

FIGURE 2.1

CUSUM SQUARES TEST FOR EQUATION (10)

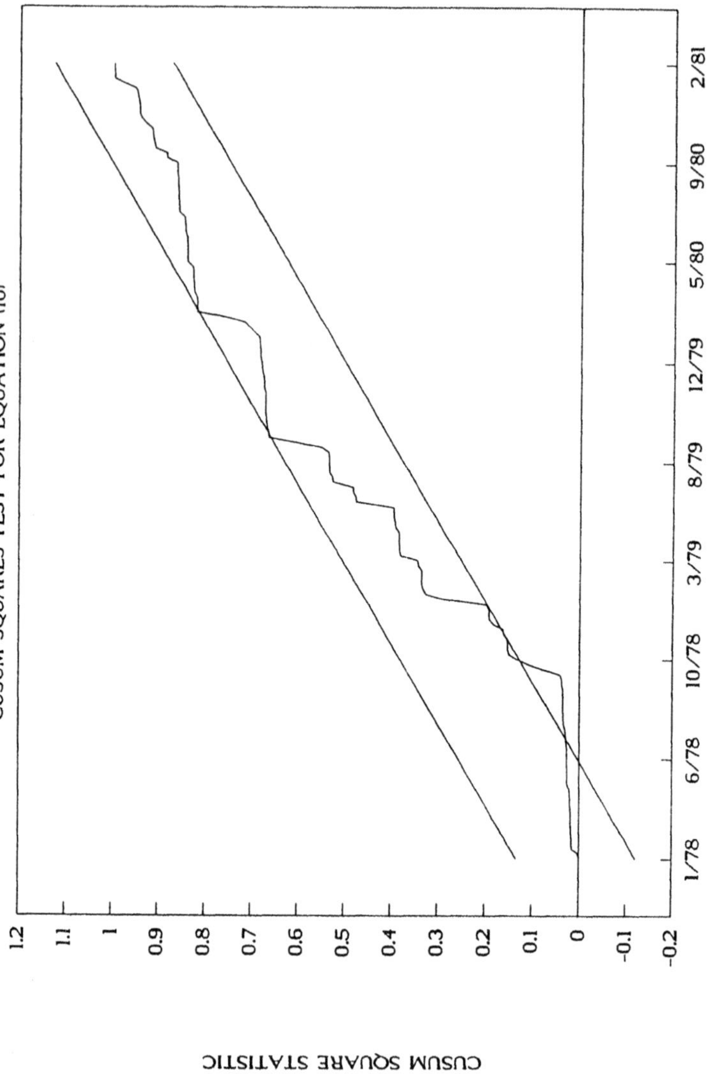

FIGURE 2.2

TIME VARYING SLOPE PARAMETER ESTIMATES FOR EQUATION (10)

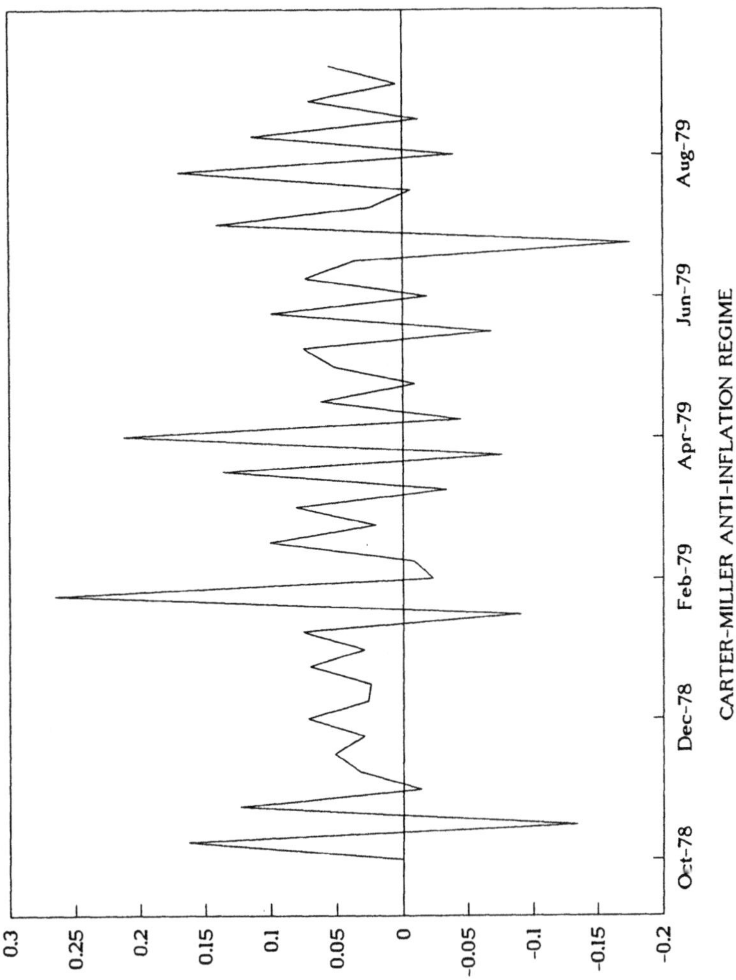

FIGURE 2.3

TIME VARYING SLOPE PARAMETER ESTIMATES FOR EQUATION (10)

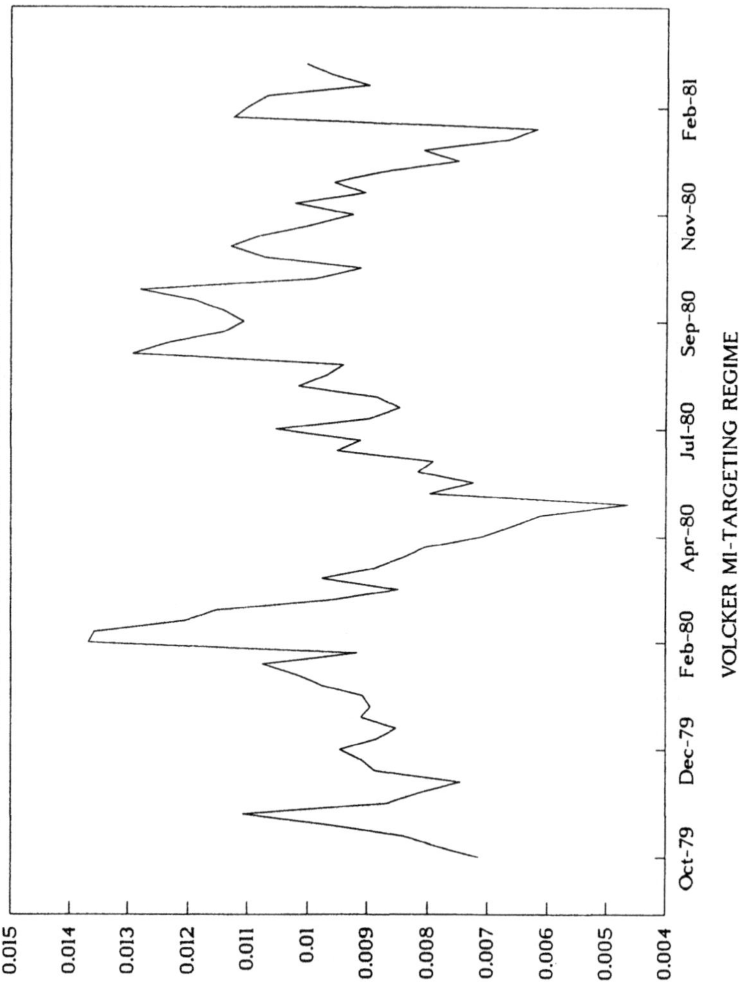

NOTES

1. Open-economy portfolio balance models are based on Tobin's (1969) financial analysis of the closed economy.

2. There exists no absolute constraints on the amount of sterilized intervention central banks can pursue. But in order to support the dollar, a central bank needs reserves of other currencies with which to purchase (and thus add to the demand for) dollars. Central banks typically enter into swap arrangements with other central banks to acquire the needed reserves. Technically, a swap consists of a simultaneous spot and forward exchange transaction. The Fed sells dollars spot to the Bundesbank for DM and simultaneously contracts to buy the dollars forward for the same amount of DM on or before a specified maturity date (which is typically set at three months with the option of rolling over an additional three months if necessary). Therefore, although in principle a central bank has no budget constraint, in practice it is limited by its swap line arrangements.

3. See Mussa (1976) for the derivation of equation (1).

4. If intervention were not sterilized, then I_t would enter directly in the vector of driving variables in (1), since a non-sterilized intervention, by definition, affects the monetary base.

5. This result depends on the assumption of sticky goods prices in the short-run. In deriving equation (1) purchasing power parity was assumed to hold instantaneously. If PPP holds only in the long run, the change in the exchange rate involves two additional terms: the expected convergence of the exchange rate to its equilibrium (PPP) path, and the spillover (or overshooting) effect of unexpected changes in the equilibrium goods price onto the exchange rate (see Dornbusch (1976), Mussa (1982)).

6. Ross (1977), for example, acknowledges that firms' managers could simply predict their future values, and be liable for the consequences of imperfect prediction. But he argues that the need for signalling (in his case by debt commitment) is driven by the fact that such verbal

commitments are difficult to interpret and enforce, and thus a more formal tie between policy choice, incentives, and performance is necessary.

7. In other words, the Treasury may perceive short-term gains from targeting even given the long-run costs associated with the policy, if non-market (political) considerations outweigh short-term efficiency goals.

8. Alternatively, we can assume that the Fed always signals informatively and it is only the Treasury that initiates targeting policy. But the market does not know *ex ante* which agency has initiated the day's policy.

9. Here it is assumed that the Fed cannot enter the market with such a large volume of reserves that it would move the market by brute force. This assumption is realistic in the sense that, although the Fed has on occasion intervened heavily, the dollar amount is small, relative to the overall size of the foreign exchange market. This assumption is also consistent with the tests of the portfolio balance model of exchange rate determination cited in the introduction.

10. The two implicit assumptions here are that the central bank knows other central banks' monetary policies, and that only the relative money supplies between countries matter in determining the exchange rates.

11. The formulation of this game is analogous to Backus and Driffill's (1985) and Barro's (1986) inflation/output game.

12. In each period of the game the equilibrium concept is Nash, but in any given period, the players take into account their strategies in future periods. Using this sequential equilibrium concept (see Kreps and Wilson (1982)), we avoid the time-inconsistent behavior that arises when policy is viewed as an optimal control problem (see Kydland and Prescott (1977)).

13. The form of the payoff function is analogous to that introduced by Barro and Gordon (1983), and has since been used in a number of papers that examine the Fed's inflation/output game. Here, however, the Fed's objective function should not be interpreted in terms of social welfare, but rather in terms of political-preferences (or pressures). The first quadratic

term on the right-hand-side implies that the Fed considers large deviations in pre- and post-announcement spot rates (large jumps) to be particularly costly.

14. Barro and Gordon (1983) show that if $0<\beta<1$ and the game is infinite, the Nash equilibrium is not unique. The reason is that the Fed's benefit from surprising the market in period t is exactly equal to the cost that occurs in t+1 when the market no longer believes the signal. With a discount factor less than one, the cost (that comes later) will be less than the benefit. In general, in infinite games with discounting, a necessary condition for a reputational equilibria to exist is that, the market's "punishment period" must be severe enough to offset the discount factor. Here, however, the game is finite; the Fed's reputation falls to zero as soon as it targets. In this game, therefore, the role of the discount factor is to value reputation. A high discount factor lessens the value of reputation and implies a shorter game.

15. While the Fed and individual investors are assumed to have different objective functions, in some circumstances it may be that the market's objective, in aggregate, is consistent with that of the Fed. If the current spot rate is not based on fundamental value, for example, the Fed's target (if chosen appropriately and believed) might remedy the misalignment (see Williamson (1983)). So while an individual would not want to be fooled by the Fed into taking a spot position consistent with the target, she might be better off if the market were to get off the bubble path.

16. Note that, although individual investors are not assumed to set their expectations strategically, investors in aggregate have a strategic effect on the Fed's intervention decisions.

17. If the Fed targets, the payoffs are derived by first maximizing Δs_t in (5) given Δs^e_t; then substituting this result, $\Delta s_t=\lambda_2/2\lambda_1$ and $\Delta s^e_t=0$ if the market is fooled or $\Delta s^e_t=\lambda_2/2\lambda_1$ otherwise, back in (5). If the Fed signals truthfully, payoffs are derived by substituting, in (5), $\Delta s_t=0$ and $\Delta s^e_t=0$ if the market believes the signal and $\Delta s^e_t=\lambda_2/2\lambda_1$ otherwise.

18. As with equation (5), here it is assumed that the market does not discount the future (ie. $\beta=1$).

19. In more realistic terms, the cost to the Fed involves loss of foreign reserves as the market bets against the signal, as well as a larger exchange rate jump at the time of the announcement.

20. See Canzoneri (1985) and Cukierman and Meltzer (1986) for examples of games that allow for incomplete (monetary) policy control. Cukierman and Meltzer show that, in some circumstances, imperfect policy control can be advantageous for policymakers. If the public cannot distinguish between changes in policy objectives and control errors, the policymaker is more likely to be able to surprise the public. In contrast, Canzoneri's reputational resolution to the problem of imperfect policy control leads to a worse off position for policymakers. Canzoneri's solution concept depends on the assumption that the market can coordinate on a threshold value for observed deviations from zero (inflation) that will deter the Fed from cheating. In equilibrium, the Fed will never cheat, but in periods of large control errors the market will nevertheless punish the Fed by reverting to high inflation expectations.

21. Canzoneri (1985, p.1061) also brings up this possible resolution.

22. Money supply announcements were not included in this exercise, as they are not direct statements of Fed policy intentions.

23. It is possible that the announcement effects on the one-day change in exchange rates are subsequently offset. However, as long as exchange-rates are best described as a random walk, any change in rates is optimally viewed as permanent rather than transitory, implying no expected future offset. Another way of looking at this is that a future offset would imply the existence of a trading rule, conditional on announcements, that violates semi-strong form market efficiency.

24. Although intervention data were available through March 1985, active U.S. intervention ceased between February 1981 and early 1985. However, due to the small sample of intervention observations in early 1985, tests only cover the period 1977 to February 1981.

25. A recursive residual is defined as the one-period-ahead forecast error at time t, based on a regression calculated using observations 1 through t-1.

26. The test is described in detail in Watson (1980) and Watson and Engle (1985).

27. The TVP models were estimated using *Forecast Master* software. The maximum likelihood solutions were found using the EM and GN algorithms sequentially.

28. See Adams and Henderson (1983) for a detailed definition of customer transactions.

29. The H.6 was released on Thursday at 4:10pm until January 31, 1980. Beginning February 8, 1980 the time was changed to Friday at 4:10pm and on February 16, 1984 the time was returned to Thursday at 4:10pm. The definition of M1 was also temporarily changed to M1-B from February 8, 1980 to January 8, 1982.

30. The expectations data, collected by telephone each week by Money Market Services of Belmont, California, have been the subject of numerous empirical investigations, that have generally shown them to be rational. See Grossman (1981), Urich and Wachtel (1981), Shiller, Campbell and Schoenholtz (1983).

31. See Cornell (1982), Engel and Frankel (1984), Hardouvelis (1984) and Hakkio and Pearce (1985).

32. If interest and exchange rates react to the money supply announcement despite preceding intervention, this implies that intervention does not convey *complete* information about the implications of the surprise.

33. Thanks to Craig Hakkio for providing me with the MMS data.

34. The 10% significance value for 158 degrees of freedom (T=160, k=2, m'=79, and n=78) in Durbin's Table 1 is c_o=0.11208.

35. The forecast test measures the increase in the goodness-of-fit that is obtained by fitting the model to data that occur after the pre-specified shift-date.

36. Alternative shift dates over the period 3/80-5/80 were tested to check shift-date sensitivity. As the alternative dates did not produce a significant Chow or Forecast test statistic, these results are not included in the table.

37. Because it is possible that the variance of the disturbances in (10) might be larger for large-intervention events (i.e. $E(v_{t,2}^2 \mid I_{t,2}) = g(I_{t,2})$), White's (1980) asymptotically consistent covariance matrix for heteroskedasticity of unknown form was used in estimating (10). White shows that given satisfaction of the other OLS assumptions, consistent estimates of the diagonal elements of the variance-covariance matrix of error terms can be generated by replacing the ith diagonal element with the ith squared residual. The heteroskedasticity-consistent covariance matrix estimator is $(X'X/T)^{-1}\hat{V}(X'X/T)^{-1}$ where $\hat{V} = T^{-1} \Sigma \hat{v}_{tT}^2 X_t'X_t$.

38. Previous time-series studies of the relationship between intervention policy and exchange rates include: Loopesko (1984) and Rogoff (1983). See Green (1984a,b) for examples of intervention case studies.

39. A number of authors have found evidence that the forward rate is a biased predictor of the future spot rate (Bilson (1981), Cumby and Obstfeld (1981, 1984), Hansen and Hodrick (1980, 1983)). Fama (1984) and Hodrick and Srivastava (1986) find evidence that the variance of the risk premium is greater than the variance of the expected rate of depreciation, implying that the risk premium may explain much of the bias in the forward rate. Frankel and Froot (1987), however, find that using survey data to proxy for expectations, the relative size of the variance is reversed. The debate over forward market efficiency remains unresolved.

40. Overlapping weekly observations were used to increase the sample size. The effective sample size with overlapping data will, however, be smaller than the actual number of weekly observations.

41. In a series of subsequent papers, I have further tested the signalling hypothesis using U.S. and German intervention data in the 1980s (Dominguez (1990a,b), Dominguez and Frankel (1992a,b)). Intervention policy in the 1980s is also examined by Obstfeld (1990).

CHAPTER 3

The Pricing of Foreign Exchange Risk in the Stock Market: A Test for International Economic Interdependence

I. INTRODUCTION

The degree of openness of any national economy is an important issue for international economic theory and policy. For example, in the 1960's, it was typically assumed that the U.S. was sufficiently large, and its economy sufficiently protected, that exogenous economic shocks from other countries did not have an important effect on U.S. macroeconomic performance. Most macroeconomic models reflected this view by representing the U.S. as a closed economy. By the early 1980's, most observers considered the U.S. to be no longer sufficiently isolated to merit this closed-economy assumption. But there has remained disagreement about the degree to which shocks originating outside the U.S. affect U.S. output and terms of trade.

Measuring the degree of openness in any national economy has proven a difficult problem. Part of the problem is the ambiguity of the term "openness". An open economy might simply be defined as one in which trade flows represent a substantial portion of net national product. But this does not capture adequately the meaning of openness as it is often used in both theory and policy. For example, many economies that are open, as measured by trade flows, are also closed to foreign competition as a matter of policy. Examples are several of the

Asian economies such as that of South Korea, that export to world markets but impose high barriers on imports.

This chapter presents a new set of empirical tests examining the openness of the U.S. economy since 1980, tests that rest upon an alternative definition of openness. The domestic economy is defined as open if its real economic welfare is significantly affected by shifts in other countries' aggregate real economic activity. This definition captures the intuitive notion of underlying economic interdependence, asking whether the economy is systemically influenced by economic changes outside its own borders. The tests examine the openness of the U.S. economy by analyzing the behavior of U.S. asset returns. The tests ask whether real other-country economic shocks, transmitted to the U.S. through exchange rate movements, generate non-diversifiable risk in U.S. asset markets.

This definition of openness, along with the asset-based approach to testing for non-diversifiable risk, allow a particularly strong test for economic interdependence across the economy. If exchange rate risk is priced, this indicates that the home-country economy is sufficiently open that no sector is impervious to changes in international economic conditions. This is stronger evidence of economic interdependence than can be provided by a structural examination concentrating (for example) on a sector-by-sector examination of trade flows. If the methodology used in this chapter shows a pricing relationship, this indicates that all sectors are affected by international conditions regardless of their trade patterns.

The tests rely on an empirical version of the Arbitrage Pricing Theory. The APT suggests that the expected cross-sectional returns on assets at any time t are functions of a finite set of common factors, each of which constitutes a source of non-diversifiable economic risk. Several domestic factors have been identified in prior tests of the APT, including changes in industrial production, and the degree of risk aversion as proxied by the difference between low-grade bonds and long term government securities. To examine the susceptibility of the U.S. economy to other-country shocks, I test whether changes in exchange rates (specifically the mark-dollar rate) are a source of non-diversifiable risk within the framework of a three-factor APT.

The tests use two controls for home-country (U.S.) shocks that might be responsible for exchange rate shifts. First, the model includes two factors that should together pick up most important shifts in home-country economic prospects: the equal-weighted market index, and interest rates. Interest rate changes should reflect shifts in monetary policy (or expectations about monetary policy) that might affect exchange rates. The equal-weighted market index should move in response to any significant change in expectations about domestic output.[1] Second, I also test whether the exclusion of important macroeconomic factors, that cannot be included in the model due to lack of daily data (an example is industrial production) bias the results of the estimates. These tests together help to ensure that any effect arising from changes in exchange rates reflects underlying shifts in non-U.S., as opposed to U.S., economic performance.

Overall, the tests show that, since 1980, changes in the mark-dollar exchange rate have been a source of non-diversifiable risk in U.S. asset markets. The exchange rate is priced in the sense of the APT: higher exchange rate exposure is associated with higher expected returns. The relationship holds throughout the six-year period examined, and in sub-periods. Moreover, the specification tests performed show that this result is robust. It is not likely to be induced by omitted variable bias; nor is it likely to reflect a general misspecification of the estimated APT model.

The chapter proceeds as follows. Section II describes the APT test framework and the empirical methodology. Section III presents results. Section IV presents tests for specification bias and robustness. Section V presents conclusions.

II. METHODOLOGY

Part A of this section presents a general overview of the APT. Part B discusses using the APT to test for international economic interdependence. Part C describes the specification of the empirical tests. Part D describes the test methodology and Part E describes the data.

A. An Overview of the APT

The APT assumes that capital markets are competitive and frictionless; that the rate of return on any security is a linear function of k factors, or

$$R_i = E(R_i) + \beta_{i1}F_1 + \ldots + \beta_{ik}F_k + \mu_i \tag{1}$$

where R_i is the (random) rate of return on the ith asset, E() is the expectations operator, β_{ik} is the covariance of the ith asset's returns and the kth factor, F_k is the kth (zero mean) factor, common to all returns, μ_i is a random noise term for the ith asset, $E(\mu_i)=0$; and that individuals know and believe that (1) is the correct description of the returns generating process. The intuition of the APT is based on the concept of arbitrage portfolios; portfolios that use no wealth, and are riskless, earn zero average returns. The first condition, that in forming a portfolio an individual can use no wealth (i.e., to buy an asset you must sell another asset), can be written as

$$\sum_{i=1}^{N} \omega_i = 0 \tag{2}$$

where ω_i is the change in the dollar amount invested in the ith asset, as a percentage of an individuals' total invested wealth, and N is the total number of assets in the portfolio. Equation (1) can now be rewritten in terms of portfolio returns by aggregating across N assets, to give

$$R_p = \sum \omega_i E(R_i) + \sum \omega_i \beta_{i1} F_1 + \ldots + \sum \omega_i \beta_{ik} F_k + \sum \omega_i \mu_i \tag{3}$$

The second condition, that the arbitrage portfolio be riskless, requires that (a) percentage changes in ω_i are small, (b) the number of assets (N) is large[2] relative to the number of common factors, (c) ω_i is chosen so that, for each factor k, the weighted sum of the systematic risk components, β_k, is zero ($\Sigma\omega_i\beta_{ik} = 0$). The requirement that the arbitrage portfolio use no wealth, and eliminate both systematic and unsystematic risk, ensures that equilibrium arbitrage portfolio returns be zero.

$$R_p = \sum \omega_i E(R_i) = 0 \tag{4}$$

Ross (1976) shows that if (4) is to hold (and $\Sigma\omega_i=0$, $\Sigma\omega_i\beta_{ik}=0$, $\Sigma\omega_i\mu_i=0$), the expected returns vector must be a linear combination of the constant vector and the vector of coefficients on the k factors.

$$E(R_i) = \alpha_0 + \alpha_1\beta_{i1} + \ldots + \alpha_k\beta_{ik} \tag{5}$$

Further, if there exists a riskless asset with rate of return R_f, then $R_f=\alpha_0$. Rewriting (5) in terms of excess returns (subtracting the risk free rate) gives,

$$E(R_i) - R_f = \alpha_1\beta_{i1} + \ldots + \alpha_k\beta_{ik} \tag{6}$$

The coefficient α_k in (6) can be interpreted as representing the risk premium on the kth factor. More generally, let δ_k be the expected return on a portfolio with unit sensitivity to the kth factor and zero sensitivity to all other factors. The risk premium, α_k, is then equal to the difference between δ_k and the risk free rate R_f, or,

$$E(R_i)-R_f = (\delta_1-R_f)\beta_{i1} + \ldots + (\delta_k-R_f)\beta_{ik} \tag{7}$$

B. The APT and International Economic Risk

Solnik (1983) has analyzed whether the traditional APT, as expressed in (7), can accommodate international capital markets. He has shown that, as long as expectations are homogeneous, capital markets are integrated and there exist risk-free assets in all currencies, any arbitrage portfolio that is nominally riskless will be riskless for any foreign investor. And, more generally, the same k factor model and pricing relationship will apply, no matter in which currency returns are measured. This implies that the IAPT (International Arbitrage Pricing Theory) is invariant to the chosen numeraire currency[3].

The tests in this chapter do not directly examine the numeraire invariance proposition[4]. Rather, the tests examine a different proposition: whether other-country economic shocks, transmitted to the home-country through exchange rate movements, are priced in home-country asset markets. Empirically it has been found that exchange rate changes fail to conform to restrictions implied by purchasing power parity (PPP). This suggests that, even if all nominal exchange rate risk could be eliminated by indexing contracts, there would remain real exchange rate risk caused by relative price fluctuations. The idea that unanticipated changes in the relative price of U.S. goods caused by other-country economic shocks are a source of business risk is not controversial. The question of whether this risk is non-diversifiable, however, has not previously been explored. It is this question that the tests in this chapter attempt to resolve.

A simple two-country example can illustrate how a negative shock in one country is transmitted to the other country through exchange rates, making both countries worse off.[5] It is in this way that exchange rate movements become a source of non-diversifiable risk. Consider a world consisting of two countries, the U.S. and Germany, and two goods, white and rye bread. Each country has a domestic industry that produces both kinds of bread. The industry in each country is publicly held and priced in an efficient market. Consumers in both countries purchase both breads, but U.S. consumers purchase relatively more white bread loafs and German consumers purchase more rye than white bread loafs. Transportation is costless and instantaneous, so goods market arbitrage guarantees that the relative price of white and rye bread must be unity. Finally, assume that initially the DM/$ exchange rate is also one.

Now consider the effect, on the exchange rate[6], of an exogenous negative shock to the rye harvest in Germany, assuming that both countries adjust their monetary policies to keep the local currency price of bread consumption unchanged after the shock.[7] The price of rye bread will be expected to rise in both countries, relative to the price of white bread, in reaction to the decrease in rye bread supply, all else remaining equal. An increase in the price of rye should, in turn, be expected to result in a decrease in rye consumption in both the U.S. and Germany (assuming that rye bread is not a Giffen good). We have assumed that the cost of U.S. and German bread consumption in local terms will be held constant by the two respective governments through changes in monetary policy. The government offset, however, will be greater in Germany because rye consumption is greater in Germany. This implies that the cost of German bread consumption must rise in terms of dollars (we have assumed it cannot rise in terms of DM). Further, goods market arbitrage ensures that bread consumption in both countries, after conversion for the exchange rate, must cost the same amount. Therefore, the price of dollars must fall relative to the price of DM.[8]

This simple example illustrates how a shock, emanating from Germany, that affects relative prices will impose income effects on consumers in both countries. In the new equilibrium real income, real consumption and real profits will be lower, and hence the market value of producing firms in both countries will also be lower. Thus the example shows that stock returns in each country will reflect the risk of shocks to the other countries' production. It is in this way that other-country economic shocks constitute a source of nondiversifiable home-country financial risk. Exchange rates are not the source of this risk but rather part of the equilibrating mechanism.

In order to test whether a premium is paid to compensate investors for bearing the risk of exchange rate changes induced by other-country shocks, it is necessary to specify a model of the returns-generating process. The APT model is used in this chapter for this task. The tests are thus tests of the joint hypothesis that the returns-generating process can be described by a linear function of a set of common factors, and that one of these factors is the innovation in the exchange rate.

C. Test Specification

The empirical model of the APT can be derived by substituting (7) into (1):

$$R_i = R_f + (\delta_1 - R_f)\beta_{i1} + \ldots + (\delta_k - R_f)\beta_{ik} + \beta_{i1}F_1 + \ldots + \beta_{ik}F_k + \mu_i \qquad (8)$$

Tests based on (8) are difficult to implement in practice. The first step is to isolate all "true" factors. The APT is then validated if (1) the risk-free rate is equal to the true risk-free rate; (2) all "true" factors are priced; and (3) no "false" factors (such as idiosyncratic firm risk) are priced. Until recently, tests based on the APT have typically employed factor analysis to extract the "true" factors. The empirical variance-covariance matrix from the returns data is computed, and a maximum-likelihood factor analysis procedure is used to identify the factors and their factor loadings, the β_is. Dhrymes, Friend and Gultekin (1984) have shown that factor analysis is extremely sensitive both to stock selection criteria and sample size. But perhaps the major frustration with this approach is that the isolated factors are not interpretable.

An alternative approach to factor analysis, used here and recently employed by Chan, Chen and Hsieh (1985) and Chen, Roll and Ross (1986), is to specify *ex ante* observable common factors based on economic theory. The appeal of this approach is that it allows interpretation of both the factor loadings and the estimated risk premia. The problem with selecting factors *ex ante* is that, in practice, it may not be possible to identify all "true" factors, and to quantify them with reliable data. Omitted variables will bias the coefficient estimates if they are not orthogonal to the included variables; further, omitted variables reduce the variance of the estimates below their efficient values. Omitted variables are particularly likely to bias the constant term. In Section IV, I examine the sensitivity of the results presented in the next section to bias from left-out variables.

The selection of factors to be included in the tests to follow was driven in large part by the availability of data. The central observable (and constraining) factor is the exchange rate. Changes in the exchange rate are used to proxy for unanticipated shifts in the relative performance of the U.S. economy. Prior to 1973, exchange rates were not market determined, and, therefore, were unlikely to reflect such shifts over the short-term. Further, extensive government intervention by the major central banks in the mid and late 1970s[9] preclude the use of this period of heavily managed--but floating-exchange rates. The tests, therefore, employ daily data over the most recent six-year period, spanning 1980-1985.[10]

Given that I am constrained to daily data, the choice of factors entering the returns generating function is limited to financial variables. I include three factors: returns on the equal-weighted NYSE index, changes in interest rates and changes in exchange rates. The equal-weighted index is included, as it has been in previous APT tests, both to reduce the probability of misspecification and to nest the prediction of the traditional CAPM model. If CAPM holds, then, with the index included, no other factor should be significant. The equal-weighted index is given "equal weight" with the other factors in the regressions. Chen, Roll and Ross term this a "fair" trial of the CAPM versus the APT, because it gives each variable the same *a priori* opportunity to be significant.[11] Three-month Treasury Bill rate changes are included to control for changes in domestic financial conditions that may simultaneously affect exchange rates. The exchange rate used in the tests is the mark/dollar rate.[12] This rate is considered the "bellwether" currency in the European Monetary System. Further, by triangular arbitrage, changes in this rate should reflect important changes in other bilateral rates, such as the mark/yen rate.[13]

Because of the small number of included variables, Section IV presents two tests of the importance of specification bias. First, I examine the bias introduced in the coefficient estimates by the failure to include the two priced domestic factors isolated in previous studies (changes in industrial production and the degree of risk aversion as measured by the yield difference between low grade bonds and long term government securities). Second, I examine whether firm-specific risk is priced in the model. A significant factor loading on firm-specific risk would indicate an important misspecification (or, alternatively, constitute a rejection of the APT).

D. Test Methodology

This chapter uses the two-stage cross-sectional approach to testing asset pricing models developed by Fama and MacBeth (1973). Observed stock market returns are employed to estimate coefficients that can then be used to test the expected returns relationship shown in equation (7).[14]

Time series estimates of the covariance of the ith asset's returns and each factor, the β_is, are first obtained over an initial period (e.g. year one) from an OLS regression of the form,

$$R_{it} = \beta_{i0} + \beta_{i1}F_{1t} + \beta_{i2}F_{2t} + \ldots + \beta_{ik}F_{kt} + \epsilon_{it} \tag{9}$$

These β_is then become the independent variables in period-by-period cross-sectional OLS regressions in the following year (year two),

$$R_i = \alpha_0 + \alpha_1\beta_{i1} + \alpha_2\beta_{i2} + \ldots + \alpha_k\beta_{ik} + \eta_i \tag{10}$$

These steps are repeated yearly[15] so as to obtain a time series of cross-sectional estimates of premiums, $\alpha_{1t},\ldots,\alpha_{kt}$. The time series means of these premia estimates can then be tested for significant difference from zero.

To correct for the errors-in-variables problem caused by using *ex post* observed returns, I adopt the approach of constructing portfolios of stocks using an *ex ante* sampling rule.[16] The task is to disperse firms' expected returns, thus averaging away the errors in variables for any specific firm, while not biasing the tests by bunching positive and negative sampling errors within portfolios. In addition to minimizing the errors-in-variables problem, the portfolio approach also addresses a second important methodological problem--the difficulty of observing factor loadings accurately in individual securities with low factor sensitivities. Forming portfolios on the basis of an *ex ante* rule that groups firms with similar expected factor exposure minimizes the problems introduced by low factor loadings and noisiness in individual firm returns.[17]

In the following empirical work, equal-weighted portfolios were formed based on two digit SIC codes, as discussed in Stambaugh (1982) and used in Sweeney and Warga. Intuition suggests that particular industries should tend to have higher exchange rate factor loadings than others (for example, export/import industries as opposed to non-trading service industries). By forming portfolios by industry we can distinguish industries that display the greatest amount of exchange rate sensitivity, in addition to testing whether exchange rate risk influences overall returns.

E. The Data

Daily firm-specific stock returns data, and the equal-weighted market index (the proxy for the market portfolio) used in the following tests are from the data tape published by the Center for Research in Security Prices (CRSP) at the University of Chicago.[18] The returns series include dividends, and are adjusted for splits, stock dividends, and special distributions. The daily exchange rate used is the closing mark/dollar bid rate in New York as provided by the New York Federal Reserve Bank.[19] The closing rate was used to insure the closest possible alignment with the stock returns data. The daily interest rate data were obtained from the Board of Governors of the Federal Reserve Board. The reported estimates use the three-month Treasury Bill rate to proxy for the interest rate.[20]

Table 3.1 presents some descriptive statistics: a correlation matrix, and twelve autocorrelations for each of variables used in the three-factor regressions. Figures 3.1 through 3.3 present the time-series graphs of each of these variables in level form. The three-month Treasury Bill rate is specified in raw change form in the regressions, while the exchange rate is specified as the difference of logarithms.[21] The correlation matrix shows that the three independent variables are far from highly correlated. This indicates that collinearity should not be a major problem in the tests. Also presented are the first twelve autocorrelations, and their corresponding t-statistics, for the three factors over the period 1980 through 1984. Autocorrelation in the variables implies the existence of an errors-in-variables problem that will bias coefficient estimates and downward bias estimates of statistical significance. Both the equal-weighted index and the three-month Treasury Bill rate show low (.26 and .13 respectively) but significant first-order autocorrelation. There is no evidence of a seasonal factor for any of the factors.

Table 3.2 presents the breakdown of industries, by SIC code, for each of the twenty-one portfolios. The number of firms per year in each portfolio changed to reflect new stock exchange listings and delistings as recorded on the daily CRSP tape. Use of the full tape at every point in time insures that no *ex post* selection problems bias the results, as might be the case in the presence of an arbitrary rule requiring a minimum survival period for individual firms. On average, each portfolio contained an equally weighted average of 87 firms' returns, so that the total number of firms' returns included per year was approximately 1,827.

III. TESTS FOR THE EXISTENCE OF AN EXCHANGE RATE RISK PREMIUM

Table 3.3 presents OLS estimates of regression (9) for each of the 21 portfolios using the equal-weighted index, EWNY, the percentage change in the mark/dollar rate, ΔDM, and the change in the three-month Treasury Bill rate, ΔTBILL, as factors over the first estimation period. As is true in previous studies, the market index remains very important in time series regressions, even in the presence of other factors. The average coefficient on EWNY was close to unity with a t-statistic ranging between 15.85 and 56.63. The coefficient on the exchange rate factor ranged between -.28 and .13 with t-statistics ranging between .07 and 4.19.

The variation of the coefficients on the exchange rate factor across individual industry portfolios is reassuring, as the values are intuitively consistent with the implications of trade theory. Mining, paper products, chemicals, primary metals, machinery, appliances and electrical equipment, manufacturing, utilities,[22] banking and finance, and holding companies all have relatively large exchange rate coefficients. Portfolios that do not show as large exchange rate exposure include construction, food and beverage, department stores, retail trade, and real estate and insurance. This is striking, in that it shows that those industries producing traded goods, ones that are most vulnerable to foreign competition, have significant exchange rate covariation. By contrast, those industries that are less sensitive to exchange rate changes are primarily concentrated in services, which is generally thought to comprise the non-traded sector.

The results in Table 3.3 are of only limited interest, as they simply tell us whether there is significant intertemporal covariance within the industry group between returns and the exchange rate. If this risk is idiosyncratic across industries (or firms), it can be diversified away, regardless of how significant is the industry-specific effect. It is only if a linear, cross-sectional relationship exists between the raw measure of risk (beta), and all firms' returns, that risk is said to be nondiversifiable, or priced in the sense of the APT.

To test for a cross-sectional risk/return relationship, the raw returns from the 21 industry portfolios are used as dependent variables in cross-sectional regressions of the form specified by equation (10) above. The independent variables are the betas for the market, the exchange rate, and the interest rate, estimated over the previous year's return series.[23] The portfolio betas are estimated in year one (1980), and then 253 daily cross-sectional regressions are run in year two, each of which tests the cross-sectional relationship between these observed betas and the relative one-day returns associated with each portfolio during 1981. This process is repeated for each of four years. The daily coefficients from the cross-sectional regressions are then stacked to form a time series of risk premia associated with each factor. For the full period, there are 1264 daily observations of the cross-sectional risk premium associated with each factor.

Summary statistics, and tests of the significance of the daily premia for each factor, are presented in Table 3.4. The table shows the average cross-sectional premium for each factor, each year for nineteen cumulative subperiods, and for the full period. The subperiods are rolling, beginning with the first calendar quarter of the estimation period (comprising 63 observations), and then adding one calendar quarter to the accumulated sample to form each subsequent sampling period. Therefore, subperiod two is comprised of the first two calendar quarters, 1981:I and 1981:II, and subperiod three is comprised of 1981:I through 1981:III. Intuitively, the significance of the stacked, time-series of factor premia asks whether the cross-sectional risk/return relationship is stable over time.

For the full sample period 1981 to 1985 (last row of Table 3.4) the risk premium associated with the unanticipated change in the exchange rate is significant at the .01 level. This result shows that, across this time period, exchange rate risk was indeed priced in the sense of the APT. In contrast, as was also found by Sweeney and Warga (1986) using monthly data, the interest rate pricing factor is not observable across the market, perhaps due to the portfolio grouping chosen. The coefficient on the exchange rate factor for the full period is .0026. This implies that a firm with an exchange rate beta of two must yield a one-quarter percentage point higher expected return than does a firm with an exchange rate beta of one.

These tests support the hypothesis that exchange rate risk is priced, subject to the caveats about observability that were discussed in Section IIC. Table 3.3 shows that some of the 21 industry portfolios show quite low levels of exchange rate covariation. This suggests that the observability problem found by Sweeny and Warga for interest rates applies to detecting exchange rate sensitivity in some of the specified portfolios. Yet despite this problem, the cross-sectional pricing relationship holds across the full universe of CRSP firms, as measured in the 21 industry portfolios. The pricing relationship would doubtless be stronger still, were attention restricted to those firms with relatively high exchange rate sensitivity.

The coefficient on the equal-weighted market index also enters significantly in the full sample period tests, but its sign is counter-intuitive. The premium is consistently negative across the full period and subperiods, implying that higher covariation with the market yields lower expected returns. Although the Roll critique (1977) clearly applies to the interpretation of these results, this is not the relationship suggested by CAPM. Further, the coefficient on the equal-weighted index is dominated by that on the exchange rate. The degree of covariation between exchange rate changes and security returns has approximately three times the pricing impact as does the degree of covariation between the market and portfolio returns.

These results for the equal-weighted index are consistent with those found by Chen, Roll and Ross using monthly data. They hypothesize that estimated market index exposures do not explain cross sectional differences is average returns after the betas of true economic state variables have been included. They conclude that, "the 'explanatory power' of the market indices may have less to do with economics and more to do with the statistical observation that large, positively-weighted portfolios of random variables are correlated" (pp.399).

To explore further the disquieting value of the EWNY premium, the test was replicated using only the market index, parallelling the classic CAPM formulation in earlier studies. The results of the one-factor model are presented in Table 3.5. The results do not suggest that the EWNY premium in the three-factor formulation is distorted by the inclusion of the exchange rate and interest rate variables. The premium on the market index beta alone is remarkably similar in economic magnitude and statistical significance to that in the full three-factor regressions.

Table 3.5's results also show that by using daily data in the post-1980 environment, the historical CAPM relationship is rejected. While there remain the usual caveats regarding the observability of the market portfolio, this is consistent with recent evidence of Shanken (1987) and Kandel and Stambaugh (1987) on the observability and validity of the traditional CAPM.[24]

A final issue in interpreting the results of Table 3.4 is the magnitude of the risk-free rate, as captured by the coefficient a_0 in the cross-sectional regressions. The risk-free rate appears to be high. The coefficient implies a baseline return of about 50% per year (with a standard error of about six percent per year). As discussed previously, it is likely that omitted variables are biasing the constant term in the regressions. Alternatively, it may be that the high risk-free rate is an artifact of the sampling period. Over the period 1980-1985, the compounded annual return on the CRSP equal-weighted market portfolio was about 40%. During 1979-1985, moreover, both nominal and real interests rates attained, and then retreated from, their highest levels in this century.

Table 3.6 presents summary statistics, by year, on the average daily raw return on each of the twenty-one industry portfolios, confirming the strong baseline return across the market in this period. Daily portfolio returns appear to average somewhat more than one-tenth of one percent. This is consistent with the market's performance over the period.

IV. SPECIFICATION TESTS

This section presents specification tests that examine whether the results from the three-variable model reported in Section III are robust. Part A discusses and quantifies the potential bias from omitted variables in the tests. Part B presents tests to determine whether important factors that should not be priced in the "true" APT are in fact priced in the three-variable model specified in this chapter.

A. Omitted Variable Bias in the Three-Factor Model

The three-variable APT specification used in the preceding tests is highly restrictive, due to the data limits imposed by daily periodicity. Consequentially, there exists the possibility that omitted factors have biased the first stage beta estimates. Bias is a particular concern in this chapter's tests because of the potential proxying role played by the exchange rate. Underlying the chapter's tests is the assumption that exchange rate changes reflect shifts in non-U.S. economic performance, and that the pricing of exchange rate risk thus shows that U.S. asset markets are affected by changes in non-U.S. economic activity. But exchange rate changes may also arise from shifts in U.S. domestic economic activity. If the exchange rate is shifting primarily due to changes in intra-U.S. economic activity, then the pricing of exchange rate risk does not necessarily reveal that U.S. asset markets are affected by non-U.S. economic activity.

Omitted variable problems such as this are not usually susceptible to analysis, because variables are omitted from estimation when they are not observable. In the case of this model, however, the omitted variable problem is different. Data for other, domestic, factors exist, but are not in daily form. The availability of these data in monthly form, coupled with the availability of monthly exchange rate data, means that an estimate can be derived of the degree of bias resulting from their omission. Their impact on the power of the tests can thus be assessed.

I test the impact of the omission of two potential factors by examining the covariance between them and the factors included in the three-factor model. When a factor from the true returns generating function is left out, a part of its influence in explaining changes in asset returns will be captured by other included factors with which it is correlated. Further, the relative share of each included factor in capturing the influence of the omitted factor will be an increasing function of the degree of partial correlation between each included factor and the excluded factor. The larger the correlation of an included and the excluded factor, the larger the extent of bias in that factor's loading (beta estimate). Alternatively, if left-out-variables and included variables are orthogonal, then there will be no bias in the beta estimates for the included variables caused by the omitted factors.

I thus perform regressions in which the independent variables are the three factors included in the daily tests--exchange rate changes, interest rate changes, and the equal-weighted index--and the dependent variables are the primary domestic factors found to be priced in Chen, Roll, and Ross. They are monthly changes in industrial production (IP)[25] and the degree of risk aversion (RA), proxied by the difference between low-grade bonds and long-term government securities.[26] A high covariance between these omitted factors, that measure changes in domestic activity, and the exchange rate, would suggest that exchange rate pricing may be an artifact, reflecting only changes in U.S. economic activity that are reflected in exchange rate changes.

The regression results with t-statistics presented in parenthesis are as follows.

$$IP_t = \underset{(1.001)}{0.002} + \underset{(1.600)}{0.046}EWNY_t - \underset{(-0.443)}{0.024}\Delta DM_t + \underset{(2.893)}{0.004}\Delta TBILL_t \quad R^2 = .14$$

$$RA_t = \underset{(19.259)}{1.812} + \underset{(2.909)}{5.274}EWNY_t + \underset{(0.543)}{1.866}\Delta DM_t - \underset{(-2.362)}{0.188}\Delta TBILL_t \quad R^2 = .27$$

These regressions suggest that the loadings on both the equal-weighted index and interest rate changes may be biased by omitted variables. Interest rate changes are a statistically significant explanatory variable for both changes in industrial production and changes in the degree of risk aversion. In contrast, the regressions show the degree of covariance between the omitted factors and exchange rate innovations to be statistically insignificant; the variables are nearly orthogonal. This result suggests that the significance of the results for the exchange rate risk premium stand essentially unaffected. In other words, these tests reveal that it is unlikely that the pricing of exchange rate risk in fact reflects merely the pricing of an underlying, purely domestic, economic factor.

The power of these tests will be reduced if the covariance structure between the omitted factor(s) and the included factors is not the same for shorter periodicities as it is for longer ones. Accordingly, one further check on the above results is presented in Table 3.7. This table presents descriptive statistics on the monthly observations of the included factors for which both daily and monthly periodicities are available (the statistics for the daily data are contained in Table 3.1).[27] If, for example, daily portfolio returns are influenced by thin trading or price-adjustment rigidities, then we should expect monthly portfolio returns to behave differently.

The monthly factor means (with the monthly changes divided by 20 to make the units comparable) are similar to their daily counterparts. The standard deviations and variances of the monthly observations of the three factors are, as would be expected, lower than those for the daily observations. Correlations between changes in the 3-month Treasury Bill and both the market index and exchange rate changes are higher in the monthly data, in the latter case by almost a factor of two. In monthly form none of the factors display first-order autocorrelation, but changes in the three-month Treasury Bill rate do display significant higher-order autocorrelation.

The evidence presented in Table 3.7 does not support the hypothesis that daily and monthly observations are equivalent either for returns on the market portfolio, or for changes in the three-month Treasury Bill rate. However, for exchange rate changes, the data do appear to be equivalent statistically in monthly and daily form. This suggests that the power of the left-out-variable tests presented in this section should be little compromised for the exchange rate variable, which is the one of concern for the results in this chapter.

B. Tests for Pricing of Firm-Specific Risk

A second, more general, approach to testing the adequacy of the three-factor model used in this chapter is to examine whether, in its estimated form, the model is broadly consistent with the implications of the theory on which it is premised. Specifically, one can examine whether, within the estimated model, factors are priced that are inconsistent with the Arbitrage Pricing Theory. If the model admits to influences that are inconsistent with theory, this would imply either that the theory is wrong, or that the specific empirical model estimated is inadequate. In either case, the model's implications for exchange rate pricing then could not be viewed to have any real power.

To test for general misspecification, I examine whether firm-specific, or idiosyncratic, risk is priced when it is added to the model as a fourth factor. The APT predicts that asset returns are linearly related to a finite set of common factors. A relationship between expected returns and idiosyncratic risk is antithetical to the theory, because the APT implies that investors can diversify away all risk except the risks of the economy as a whole (which are represented by the APT's common factors). Thus, if a measure of firm-specific risk is priced when added to the three-factor model, this would imply either that the empirical model is misspecified, or that the APT does not hold.

To test for pricing of firm-specific risk, the standard deviation of the least-squares residuals σ_ϵ from equation (9) was estimated annually for 1980-1984, averaged across assets in each of the 21 portfolios, and added as the fourth factor to the cross-section regressions. σ_ϵ captures that part of the dispersion of the distribution of returns on each portfolio that is orthogonal to the three included factors. Table 3.8 presents the risk premia estimates from the four-factor model. The risk premium associated with σ_ϵ is insignificant across the full period and all subperiods. In addition, risk premia on both the equal-weighted index and the exchange rate factor are not affected by the addition of σ_ϵ. The premium on the interest rate factor remains insignificant across individual years, becomes significant within some of the rolling subperiods, but remains insignificant over the full five-year period.

Overall, these results show that firm-specific risk is not priced, and that its addition to the three-factor model does not affect the risk premia on the original factors. This suggests that the estimated factor loading on exchange rate changes in the three-factor model is not the result of general misspecification. The results lend further support to the hypothesis that exchange rate risk is priced in the domestic asset market, while also validating a central tenet of the APT--that idiosyncratic risk should be fully diversifiable.

V. CONCLUSIONS

This chapter tests whether changes in economic conditions outside the U.S., as proxied by innovations in the exchange rate, are a source of significant non-diversifiable risk in the U.S. stock market. The tests use daily returns data for the universe of NYSE and AMEX firms, for the post-1980 period, to test for a relationship between exchange rate exposure and asset pricing. The model incorporates daily returns on the equal-weighted index and daily interest rate changes to control for the effects of purely domestic economic changes that might otherwise be assigned to the exchange rate.

The results of the tests confirm that exchange rate risk is priced across the market, in the sense of the APT. Higher covariation between a firm's returns and movements in the exchange rate mandate a higher expected return in order to offset the effects of increased risk from international economic shocks. The result appears to be robust with respect to both omitted-variable bias and model misspecification. The sign on the exchange rate risk premium is systematically and reliably positive over the full period and subperiods.

The industry-specific degree of exchange rate risk exposure is in keeping with intuition and empirical evidence on international trade patterns. The greatest exchange rate sensitivity is displayed by raw materials and industrial products (e.g., mining, chemicals, machinery), industries that produce traded goods and compete in world markets. In contrast, little exchange rate risk is found in goods that are typically non-traded, including construction and real estate. The market's allocation of exchange rate risk is, therefore, in keeping with economic intuition about the relative impact of international shocks on different economic sectors.

These results show that U.S. asset market's risk and return structure is influenced by the changing relative position of other world economies with which the U.S. trades and competes. In some sense, this merely confirms intuition about the current state of economic interdependence between American and foreign economies. But it is also the first systematic evidence quantifying the effect of this interdependence on asset markets.

TABLE 3.1

Descriptive Statistics (Daily Factors)

(January 1980 to December 1984)

	MEAN*100	STD	VARIANCE
EWNY	0.08474	0.77644	0.60285
ΔDM	0.04848	0.70670	0.49943
ΔTBILL	-0.37549	22.22747	494.06060

Correlation Matrix

	EWNY	ΔDM	ΔTBILL
EWNY	1.00000		
ΔDM	-0.19707	1.00000	
ΔTBILL	-0.22618	0.27677	1.00000

Autocorrelations ρ_1 to ρ_{12}

	EWNY (t-stat)	ΔDM (t-stat)	ΔTBILL (t-stat)
ρ_1	0.25855 (9.11)	-0.04281 (1.51)	0.13492 (4.75)
ρ_2	0.03126 (1.06)	0.04679 (1.64)	0.02107 (0.74)
ρ_3	0.04831 (1.64)	0.04461 (1.56)	-0.03801 (1.32)
ρ_4	-0.02791 (0.95)	-0.01828 (0.64)	0.05076 (1.77)
ρ_5	0.07328 (1.49)	0.03225 (1.13)	0.55814 (1.94)
ρ_6	0.02974 (1.01)	0.01561 (0.55)	-0.00225 (0.08)
ρ_7	0.00118 (0.04)	-0.01222 (0.43)	-0.00891 (0.31)
ρ_8	0.01599 (0.54)	0.00557 (0.19)	0.04663 (1.63)
ρ_9	0.00191 (0.06)	0.01553 (0.55)	0.02255 (0.79)
ρ_{10}	-0.00523 (0.17)	0.04422 (1.55)	0.02328 (0.81)
ρ_{11}	-0.03780 (1.29)	0.00243 (0.08)	0.00532 (0.18)
ρ_{12}	0.02742 (0.97)	-0.02432 (0.85)	0.00658 (0.23)

EWNY = daily return on the equal weighted NYSE index (CRSP)
DM = log of daily NY closing DM/$ exchange rate (FRNY)
TBILL = daily 3-month Treasury Bill rate (FRB)
Δ = daily change

TABLE 3.2

Industry Portfolios

Firms on the daily CRSP tape were placed into 21 industry portfolios on the basis of the Standard Industry Classification (SIC).

Industry	Portfolio	SIC code	avg # of firms*
1.	Mining	10-14	128
2.	Construction	15-17	29
3.	Food and Beverage	20	66
4.	Textile and Apparel	22,23	75
5.	Paper Products	26	38
6.	Chemical	28	107
7.	Petroleum	29	27
8.	Stone, Clay and Glass	32	38
9.	Primary Metals	33	54
10.	Fabricated Metals	34	76
11.	Machinery	35	141
12.	Appliances, Electrical	36	162
13.	Transportation Equipment	37	74
14.	Manufacturing	38,39	83
15.	Other Transportation	41,42,44,45,47	59
16.	Utilities	49	158
17.	Department Stores	53	34
18.	Retail Trade	50-52,54-59	175
19.	Banking and Finance	60	77
20.	Real Estate and Insurance	63-66	59
21.	Holding Companies	67	172

* The number of firms per year in each industry portfolio changed to reflect new American and New York stock exchange listings and delistings as recorded on the daily CRSP tape.

TABLE 3.3

Portfolio Beta Estimates

Daily time-series betas and t-statistics from regressions of industry portfolio returns (P1 to P21) on the equal-weighted index (EWNY), innovations in the mark/dollar rate (ΔDM), and innovations in the three-month Treasury Bill rate (ΔTBILL) over the period January 1980 through December 1980.

$$R_{pt} = \beta_{p0} + \beta_{p1}EWNY_t + \beta_{p2}\Delta DM_t + \beta_{p3}\Delta TBILL_t + \epsilon_{pt}$$

	β_{p0} (t-stat)	β_{p1} (t-stat)	β_{p2} (t-stat)	β_{p3} (t-stat)
P1	.0002 (0.27)	1.68 (26.15)	-0.28 (2.75)	0.005 (2.37)
P2	.0003 (0.83)	1.14 (27.37)	-0.05 (0.79)	-0.001 (0.42)
P3	-.0003 (1.30)	0.85 (35.21)	-0.06 (1.48)	-0.001 (0.28)
P4	.0001 (0.00)	0.77 (27.10)	0.01 (0.22)	0.001 (0.76)
P5	-.0004 (1.55)	0.83 (29.60)	0.09 (1.96)	-0.001 (0.88)
P6	-.0002 (0.93)	1.01 (52.12)	0.09 (3.06)	-0.001 (0.87)
P7	-.0001 (0.17)	1.32 (15.85)	-0.01 (0.07)	-0.001 (0.44)
P8	.0002 (0.59)	0.72 (23.62)	0.08 (1.57)	-0.001 (1.47)
P9	-.0004 (1.31)	1.16 (38.52)	0.09 (1.97)	0.001 (0.76)
P10	-.0001 (0.00)	0.98 (42.00)	0.05 (1.43)	0.001 (1.44)
P11	-.0003 (1.83)	1.13 (56.34)	0.13 (4.19)	0.001 (0.54)
P12	-.0001 (0.01)	1.28 (55.15)	0.11 (2.94)	0.001 (0.92)
P13	-.0002 (0.56)	0.99 (53.33)	0.10 (1.87)	0.001 (0.12)
P14	-.0004 (2.00)	1.25 (56.63)	0.08 (2.39)	0.001 (0.50)
P15	-.0004 (1.14)	1.13 (30.95)	0.11 (1.96)	-0.001 (0.71)
P16	.0001 (0.33)	0.53 (19.20)	-0.13 (2.96)	0.003 (3.11)
P17	-.0002 (1.26)	0.91 (51.52)	0.01 (0.22)	0.001 (0.72)
P18	-.0004 (1.46)	0.75 (24.26)	0.03 (0.64)	-0.002 (1.77)
P19	.0001 (0.07)	0.80 (27.38)	-0.14 (3.11)	-0.002 (2.24)
P20	.0001 (0.12)	0.96 (32.59)	-0.04 (0.85)	-0.002 (1.65)
P21	.0002 (1.15)	0.76 (43.18)	-0.09 (3.40)	-0.001 (2.09)

TABLE 3.4

Average 3-Factor Risk Premia Estimates

Results are for a two-step regression process, in which daily time-series estimates of βs are obtained from Step 1 regressions,

$$R_{pt} = \beta_{p0} + \beta_{p1} EWNY_t + \beta_{p2} \Delta DM_t + \beta_{p3} \Delta TBILL_t + \epsilon_{pt}$$

and then used as cross-sectional independent variables in Step 2:

$$R_p = \alpha_0 + \alpha_1 \hat{\beta}_{p1} + \alpha_2 \hat{\beta}_{p2} + \alpha_3 \hat{\beta}_{p3} + \eta_p$$

Daily coefficients for each of the independent variables from Step 2 are then stacked to form a time-series. Reported coefficients and t-statistics are for the average of these time series. See Table 3.1 for variable definitions.

Period	OBS	α_0 (t-stat)	α_1 (t-stat)	α_2 (t-stat)	α_3 (t-stat)
81-81:I	63	.0055 (4.36)	-.0037 (-2.48)	.0051 (4.02)	.4562 (3.11)
81-81:II	126	.0043 (4.82)	-.0032 (-3.27)	.0043 (3.57)	.3007 (3.01)
81-81:III	189	.0024 (3.21)	-.0024 (-2.99)	.0014 (1.39)	.1798 (2.17)
81-81:IV	252	.0019 (3.14)	-.0017 (-2.39)	.0008 (1.85)	.1139 (1.38)
81-82:I	315	.0019 (3.55)	-.0018 (-2.86)	.0019 (1.56)	.0745 (1.17)
81-82:II	378	.0018 (4.09)	-.0018 (-3.28)	.0031 (2.24)	.0971 (1.74)
81-82:III	441	.0020 (4.98)	-.0018 (-3.44)	.0027 (1.74)	.0900 (1.77)
81-83:IV	504	.0019 (5.13)	-.0012 (-2.54)	.0045 (2.65)	.0481 (1.02)
81-83:I	567	.0022 (6.25)	-.0013 (-2.76)	.0052 (3.23)	.0471 (1.13)
81-83:II	630	.0021 (6.17)	-.0009 (-2.14)	.0049 (3.21)	.0616 (1.59)
81-83:III	693	.0020 (6.18)	-.0009 (-2.25)	.0039 (2.78)	.0412 (1.14)
81-84:IV	759	.0019 (6.25)	.0009 (-2.46)	.0038 (2.79)	.0471 (1.39)
81-84:I	819	.0017 (6.19)	-.0009 (-2.55)	.0028 (2.23)	.0429 (1.36)
81-84:II	882	.0017 (6.59)	-.0009 (-3.02)	.0031 (2.59)	.0458 (1.56)
81-84:III	942	.0017 (6.64)	-.0009 (-2.77)	.0028 (2.49)	.0380 (1.38)
81-84:IV	1008	.0016 (6.76)	-.0009 (-2.98)	.0027 (2.55)	.0309 (1.20)
81-85:I	1071	.0016 (7.22)	-.0008 (-2.96)	.0024 (2.35)	.0309 (1.26)
81-85:II	1134	.0017 (7.73)	-.0009 (-3.25)	.0025 (2.56)	.0231 (0.99)
81-85:III	1197	.0016 (7.69)	-.0008 (-3.28)	.0024 (2.51)	.0274 (1.23)
81-85:IV	1264	.0017 (8.33)	-.0009 (-3.43)	.0026 (2.86)	.0269 (1.27)

TABLE 3.4 (cont.)

Average 3-Factor Risk Premia Estimates

Results are for a two-step regression process, in which daily time-series estimates of βs are obtained from Step 1 regressions,

$$R_{pt} = \beta_{p0} + \beta_{p1} EWNY_t + \beta_{p2} \Delta DM_t + \beta_{p3} \Delta TBILL_t + \epsilon_{pt}$$

and then used as cross-sectional independent variables in Step 2:

$$R_p = \alpha_0 + \alpha_1 \hat{\beta}_{p1} + \alpha_2 \hat{\beta}_{p2} + \alpha_3 \hat{\beta}_{p3} + \eta_p$$

Daily coefficients for each of the independent variables from Step 2 are then stacked to form a time-series. Reported coefficients and t-statistics are for the average of these time series. See Table 3.1 for variable definitions.

Year	OBS	α_0 (t-stat)	α_1 (t-stat)	α_2 (t-stat)	α_3 (t-stat)
1981	253	.0020 (3.25)	-.0017 (-2.45)	.0009 (1.97)	.1111 (1.47)
1982	253	.0018 (4.28)	-.0006 (-1.97)	.0082 (2.51)	.0157 (0.28)
1983	253	.0017 (3.58)	-.0003 (-1.57)	.0023 (2.00)	.0444 (1.11)
1984	253	.0008 (2.75)	-.0008 (-1.90)	.0006 (1.98)	.0167 (1.19)
1985	252	.0018 (6.30)	-.0007 (-2.00)	.0022 (2.34)	.0111 (0.46)

TABLE 3.5

Average CAPM Risk Premia Estimates

Results are for a two-step regression process, in which daily time-series estimates of βs are obtained from Step 1 regressions,

$$R_{pt} = \beta_{p0} + \beta_{p1}EWNY_t + \epsilon_{pt}$$

and then used as cross-sectional independent variables in Step 2:

$$R_p = \alpha_0 + \alpha_1\hat{\beta}_{p1} + \eta_p$$

Daily coefficients for each of the independent variables from Step 2 are then stacked to form a time-series. Reported coefficients and t-statistics are for the average of these time series. See Table 3.1 for variable definitions.

Period	OBS	α_0 (t-stat)	α_1 (t-stat)
81-81:I	63	.0036 (4.27)	-.0019 (-1.54)
81-81:II	126	.0031 (4.72)	-.0020 (-2.58)
81-81:III	189	.0017 (3.04)	-.0018 (-2.59)
81-81:IV	252	.0015 (3.43)	-.0013 (-2.26)
81-82:I	315	.0017 (4.16)	-.0017 (-2.98)
81-82:II	378	.0015 (4.30)	-.0016 (-3.06)
81-82:III	441	.0017 (5.14)	-.0015 (-3.12)
81-82:IV	504	.0020 (5.93)	-.0013 (-2.89)
81-83:I	567	.0022 (6.98)	-.0013 (-2.99)
81-83:II	630	.0020 (6.81)	-.0009 (-2.27)
81-83:III	693	.0019 (6.89)	-.0009 (-2.42)
81-83:IV	759	.0018 (6.93)	.0009 (-2.62)
81-84:I	819	.0017 (6.69)	-.0009 (-2.62)
81-84:II	882	.0016 (6.87)	-.0009 (-2.92)
81-84:III	942	.0016 (7.34)	-.0009 (-2.94)
81-84:IV	1008	.0016 (7.87)	-.0009 (-3.49)
81-85:I	1071	.0016 (8.35)	-.0009 (-3.44)
81-85:II	1134	.0017 (8.95)	-.0009 (-3.79)
81-85:III	1197	.0016 (8.81)	-.0009 (-3.78)
81-85:IV	1264	.0017 (9.52)	-.0009 (-3.92)

TABLE 3.5 (cont.)
Average CAPM Risk Premia Estimates

Results are for a two-step regression process, in which daily time-series estimates of βs are obtained from Step 1 regressions,

$$R_{pt} = \beta_{p0} + \beta_{p1}EWNY_t + \epsilon_{pt}$$

and then used as cross-sectional independent variables in Step 2:

$$R_p = \alpha_0 + \alpha_1\hat{\beta}_{p1} + \eta_p$$

Daily coefficients for each of the independent variables from Step 2 are then stacked to form a time-series. Reported coefficients and t-statistics are for the average of these time series. See Table 3.1 for variable definitions.

Year	OBS	α_0 (t-stat)	α_1 (t-stat)
1981	253	.0015 (3.52)	-.0013 (-2.28)
1982	253	.0024 (4.77)	-.0010 (-1.95)
1983	253	.0015 (3.65)	-.0002 (-1.65)
1984	253	.0011 (3.02)	-.0011 (-2.13)
1985	252	.0018 (6.39)	-.0007 (-1.97)

TABLE 3.6

Average Industry Portfolio Returns

Average daily industry portfolio returns (over 253 days) for each year.

	1980	1981	1982	1983	1984	1985
P1	.00231	-.00092	-.00028	.00124	-.00077	.00049
P2	.00182	-.00033	.00137	.00136	.00016	.00100
P3	.00082	.00054	.00153	.00127	.00054	.00167
P4	.00105	.00102	.00162	.00210	-.00031	.00145
P5	.00075	.00025	.00120	.00143	-.00012	.00125
P6	.00123	.00018	.00100	.00129	-.00003	.00139
P7	.00162	-.00080	-.00001	.00088	.00003	.00117
P8	.00116	.00013	.00110	.00134	.00014	.00119
P9	.00124	.00006	-.00014	.00173	-.00067	.00058
P10	.00135	.00008	.00078	.00147	-.00016	.00103
P11	.00124	-.00030	.00055	.00131	-.00035	.00068
P12	.00178	.00011	.00145	.00156	-.00034	.00085
P13	.00147	.00028	.00161	.00155	-.00026	.00056
P14	.00132	.00015	.00131	.00108	-.00037	.00107
P15	.00117	.00025	.00135	.00120	-.00007	.00110
P16	.00070	.00055	.00103	.00078	-.00073	.00123
P17	.00102	.00069	.00192	.00157	-.00011	.00109
P18	.00059	.00062	.00222	.00185	.00018	.00194
P19	.00099	.00041	.00141	.00109	.00013	.00152
P20	.00128	.00047	.00165	.00127	.00012	.00162
P21	.00115	.00031	.00140	.00121	.00037	.00098

TABLE 3.7

Descriptive Statistics (Monthly Factors)

(January 1980 to December 1984)

	MEAN*100/20	STD	VARIANCE
EWNY	0.06166	0.24738	0.06120
ΔDM	0.04875	0.14000	0.01960
ΔTBILL	-0.32592	6.29780	39.66247

Correlation Matrix

	EWNY	ΔDM	ΔTBILL
EWNY	1.00000		
ΔDM	-0.17508	1.00000	
ΔTBILL	-0.32414	0.47119	1.00000

Autocorrelations ρ_1 to ρ_{12}

	EWNY (t-stat)	ΔDM (t-stat)	ΔTBILL (t-stat)
ρ_1	0.14724 (0.90)	0.27182 (1.60)	0.14889 (0.99)
ρ_2	0.15816 (0.97)	-0.05994 (0.33)	-0.14361 (0.96)
ρ_3	-0.11142 (0.67)	0.08366 (0.48)	0.27022 (1.88)
ρ_4	0.08905 (0.53)	-0.03121 (0.17)	-0.24538 (1.83)
ρ_5	0.18757 (1.06)	0.06135 (0.35)	0.34432 (2.45)
ρ_6	0.02975 (0.16)	0.05338 (0.30)	-0.38853 (2.64)
ρ_7	0.13676 (0.78)	-0.01235 (0.06)	0.04419 (0.32)
ρ_8	-0.09564 (0.54)	0.13279 (0.75)	-0.12754 (1.02)
ρ_9	0.01319 (0.07)	-0.17545 (0.98)	0.34354 (2.88)
ρ_{10}	0.01789 (0.11)	0.12499 (0.71)	-0.23972 (1.95)
ρ_{11}	-0.10037 (0.65)	-0.09964 (0.55)	0.11046 (0.93)
ρ_{12}	-0.16325 (1.09)	-0.01094 (0.06)	-0.33182 (2.96)

EWNY = monthly return on the equal weighted NYSE index (CRSP)
DM = log of monthly NY closing DM/$ exchange rate (FRNY)
TBILL = monthly 3-month Treasury Bill rate (FRB)
Δ = monthly change

TABLE 3.8

Average 4-Factor Risk Premia Estimates

Results are for a two-step regression process, in which daily time-series estimates of βs and σ_ϵ are obtained from Step 1 regressions,

$$R_{pt} = \beta_{p0} + \beta_{p1}EWNY_t + \beta_{p2}\Delta DM_t + \beta_{p3}\Delta TBILL_t + \epsilon_{pt}$$

and then used as cross-sectional independent variables in Step 2:

$$R_p = \alpha_0 + \alpha_1\hat{\beta}_{p1} + \alpha_2\hat{\beta}_{p2} + \alpha_3\hat{\beta}_{p3} + \alpha_4\sigma_\epsilon + \eta_p$$

Daily coefficients for each of the independent variables from Step 2 are then stacked to form a time-series. Reported coefficients and t-statistics are for the average of these time series. All sample periods begin in 1981. See Table 3.5 for the number of observations in each subperiod.

Period	α_0 (t-stat)	α_1 (t-stat)	α_2 (t-stat)	α_3 (t-stat)	α_4 (t-stat)
81:I	.005 (4.84)	-.002 (-1.82)	.003 (2.46)	.329 (2.61)	-.175 (-1.27)
81:II	.004 (5.85)	-.002 (-2.98)	.003 (3.13)	.229 (2.60)	-.099 (-0.91)
81:III	.002 (3.79)	-.002 (-3.19)	.001 (1.37)	.138 (1.94)	-.057 (-0.67)
81:IV	.002 (3.72)	-.001 (-1.27)	.001 (2.22)	.064 (0.99)	-.064 (-0.87)
82:I	.002 (4.58)	-.002 (-2.71)	.001 (1.98)	.079 (1.42)	-.126 (-1.01)
82:II	.002 (5.07)	-.002 (-3.19)	.003 (2.04)	.099 (2.05)	-.104 (-1.85)
83:III	.002 (5.87)	-.001 (-3.33)	.002 (1.57)	.087 (1.94)	-.079 (-1.51)
83:IV	.002 (5.90)	-.001 (-2.29)	.004 (2.51)	.043 (1.02)	-.064 (-1.31)
83:I	.002 (7.17)	-.001 (-2.51)	.005 (3.02)	.090 (2.28)	-.066 (-1.38)
83:II	.002 (7.13)	-.001 (-2.06)	.004 (2.79)	.105 (2.78)	-.043 (-0.95)
83:III	.002 (7.16)	-.001 (-2.38)	.003 (2.24)	.083 (2.36)	-.027 (-0.62)
84:IV	.002 (7.17)	-.001 (2.43)	.003 (2.38)	.083 (2.51)	-.035 (-0.86)
84:I	.002 (7.01)	-.001 (-2.69)	.003 (1.99)	.075 (2.44)	-.013 (-0.34)
84:II	.002 (7.41)	-.001 (-3.22)	.003 (2.36)	.075 (2.64)	-.010 (-0.27)
84:III	.002 (7.43)	-.001 (-2.90)	.003 (2.27)	.066 (2.44)	-.008 (-0.21)
85:IV	.002 (7.49)	-.001 (-3.30)	.003 (2.45)	.056 (2.21)	.008 (0.23)
85:I	.002 (7.87)	-.001 (-3.23)	.002 (2.28)	.054 (1.99)	.012 (0.36)
85:II	.002 (8.23)	-.001 (-3.54)	.003 (2.55)	.044 (1.29)	.022 (0.71)
85:III	.002 (8.16)	-.001 (-3.57)	.002 (2.57)	.047 (1.66)	.020 (0.67)
85:IV	.002 (8.98)	-.001 (-3.71)	.003 (2.79)	.046 (1.81)	.015 (0.51)

TABLE 3.8 (cont.)
Average 4-Factor Risk Premia Estimates

Results are for a two-step regression process, in which daily time-series estimates of βs and the standard deviation of the residuals σ_ϵ are obtained from Step 1 regressions,

$$R_{pt} = \beta_{p0} + \beta_{p1}EWNY_t + \beta_{p2}\Delta DM_t + \beta_{p3}\Delta TBILL_t + \epsilon_{pt}$$

and then used as cross-sectional independent variables in Step 2:

$$R_p = \alpha_0 + \alpha_1\hat{\beta}_{p1} + \alpha_2\hat{\beta}_{p2} + \alpha_3\hat{\beta}_{p3} + \alpha_4\sigma_\epsilon + \eta_p$$

Daily coefficients for each of the independent variables from Step 2 are then stacked to form a time-series. Reported coefficients and t-statistics are for the average of these time series. See Table 3.5 (cont.) for the number of observations in each subperiod.

Year	α_0 (t-stat)	α_1 (t-stat)	α_2 (t-stat)	α_3 (t-stat)	α_4 (t-stat)
1981	.002 (3.71)	-.001 (-1.26)	.001 (2.26)	.065 (0.98)	-.064 (-0.89)
1982	.002 (4.71)	-.001 (-1.02)	.008 (2.53)	.024 (0.48)	-.072 (-1.09)
1983	.002 (4.02)	-.001 (-0.91)	.001 (2.02)	.159 (1.92)	.025 (0.33)
1984	.001 (2.45)	-.001 (-2.43)	.001 (2.46)	.025 (1.78)	.123 (1.30)
1985	.002 (5.72)	-.001 (-2.01)	.002 (2.51)	.009 (0.38)	.060 (1.15)

FIGURE 3.1

RETURN ON THE EQUAL WEIGHTED NYSE INDEX

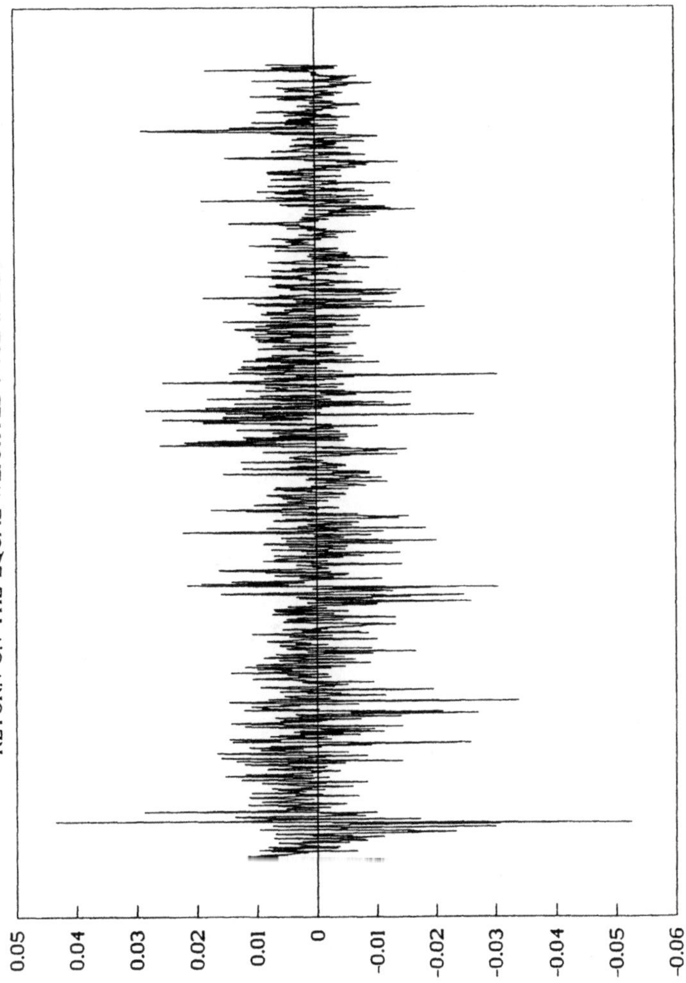

1980 - 1984

SOURCE: C.R.S.P.

FIGURE 3.2

DAILY CLOSING MARK/DOLLAR RATE

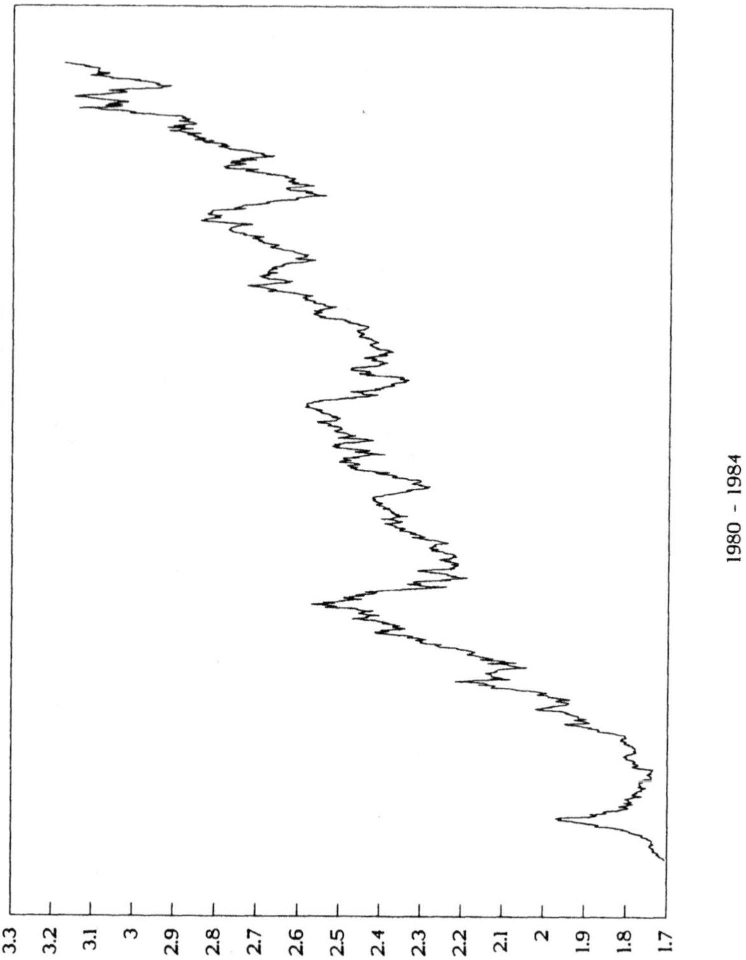

SOURCE: NYFRB

FIGURE 3.3

3-MONTH U.S. TREASURY BILL RATE

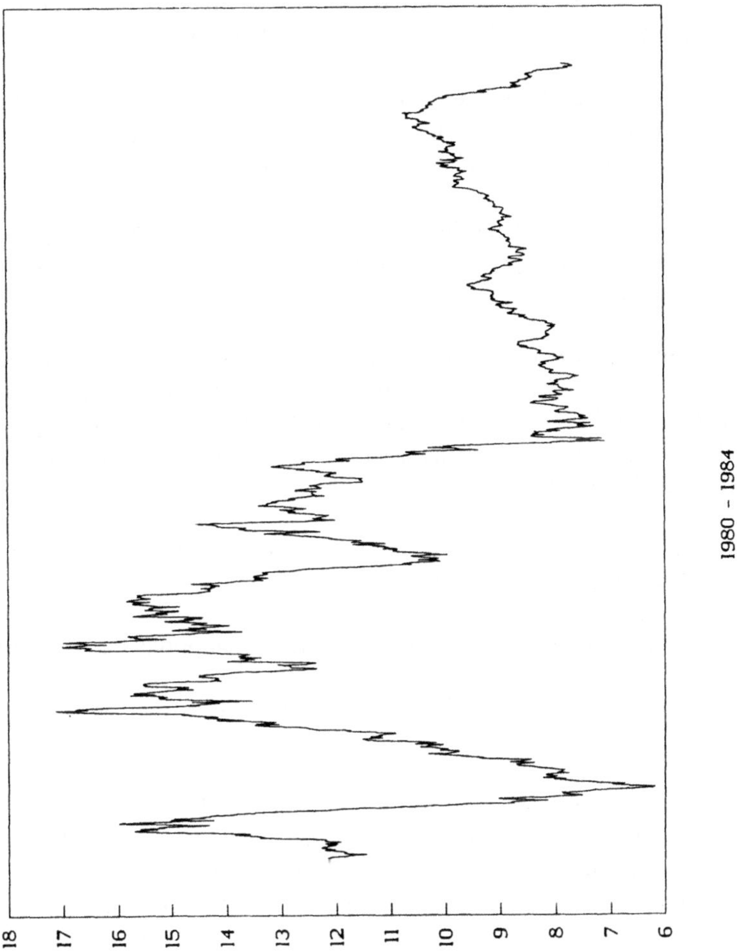

SOURCE: FRB

NOTES

1. Other empirical tests of the APT have also included the equal-weighted market index explicitly to control for omitted domestic factors.

2. The law of large numbers ensures that, in the limit, a weighted average of the error terms μ_i approaches zero ($\Sigma\omega_i\mu_i=0$); portfolio diversification thereby eliminates unsystematic risk.

3. Dollar returns of German and U.S. assets are governed by the same returns generating process (e.g., equation 1) as are mark returns of the same assets.

4. A number of authors have examined this proposition. Cho, Eun, and Senbet (1986), for example, present results that support the hypothesis that the IAPT is largely invariant to the numeraire currency chosen. However, they find that the assumption of capital market integration is rejected by the data.

5. The following example is similar in spirit to ones discussed in Solnik (1978), Cornell (1980) and Stockman (1980).

6. Relative prices must remain the same, given goods market arbitrage.

7. The point here is to abstract from inflation effects on the exchange rate.

8. It should be noted that PPP was violated in this example. PPP would imply that, in a world of no inflation, exchange rates should be constant. Here we assumed zero inflation but exchange rates did in fact change. In general, whenever consumption patterns are different across countries, PPP will be violated, because price indexes do not place the same weights on the prices of different goods.

9. See chapter 2.

10. While central banks did intervene in the foreign exchange market over this period, most visibly in September 1985 after the G-5 Plaza Agreement, the float was relatively clean in comparison to the earlier period. Between 1981 and early 1985 the Federal Reserve stopped foreign exchange intervention completely.

11. There is, of course, the risk that pricing of another factor may only indicate that the additional factor is highly correlated with the market portfolio. This possibility will be addressed in Section IV. However, it seems unlikely that this conclusion would hold for exchange rates, should they be priced.

12. Although in theory all important bilateral rates should be included in the model, in practice it was not possible to include more than one exchange rate in the regressions due to the high degree of multicollinearity between bilateral rates among countries in the G-5.

13. A possible alternative approach is to use a measure of average foreign currency strength (there are several well-known "currency basket" measures of this sort available). However, in both statistical and economic terms, it is clear that observation of a bilateral rate is more reliable than are indices that average rates across many different currencies.

14. Sweeney and Warga (1986) use an iterative FIML approach (a variant of the approach employed by Gibbons (1982)), to estimate equation (8) on SIC-coded industry portfolios. By simultaneously estimating the betas and premia they avoid the potential errors-in-variables in observed returns. In testing against the null hypothesis that $(\delta_1 - R_f) = 0$, however, the FIML standard errors have been shown to be identical to those estimated by the Fama and MacBeth technique. Mankiw and Shapiro (1986) use and present results for four different premia estimation techniques (OLS, WLS, GLS, and GLS using instrumental variables). A number of different estimation techniques were also used here, but results were similar in all cases, so only the OLS results are presented.

15. The process of estimating β_i is repeated yearly in order to offset the well documented problem of non-constancy of betas over time.

16. Blume (1970) and Black, Jensen and Scholes (1972) show that, to minimize the bias inherent in an estimate of β_i, portfolio returns rather than individual firm returns should be used. Intuitively, if the errors in the estimation of the β_is (the ϵ_{it}) are not independent from security to security, using portfolios to estimate β_ps will provide more precise estimates of the true βs by reducing (averaging) the noise in individual asset returns. A number of different criteria have been used to form such portfolios. Fama and MacBeth advocate forming portfolios from ranked β_is computed from data for a single time period, and then using a subsequent period of fresh data for estimation. Chen, Roll and Ross (1986) and Chan, Chen and Hsieh (1985) form portfolios based on firm size and Sweeney and Warga (1986) form portfolios based on two digit SIC codes.

17. The portfolio approach also contains potential pitfalls. Firms may be grouped imperfectly, and some factor sensitivities may cancel within portfolios. It may, therefore, appear that some portfolios have negligible factor loadings, although the individual firms within each portfolio do. Factor pricing across the universe of portfolio-grouped firms might thus not be detected. Sweeney and Warga, for example, report this problem in their market-wide tests for interest rate risk pricing. They find that they cannot detect a pricing effect for interest rate risk across portfolios comprising the universe of securities, presumably due to low factor loadings. They then restrict their tests to firms displaying high interest factor loadings (as measured in the time-series regressions), and demonstrate that the cross-sectional APT pricing relationship holds for this subperiod. Because APT's implications hold for any subset of the asset universe, as well as the full asset portfolio, they infer from these results that interest rate risk is indeed priced in the sense of the APT, but that it is difficult to observe across the market due to low factor loadings and portfolio composition problems.

18. The value weighted market index was also used, but as the results were virtually identical to those using the equal weighted index, the second set of results are not presented in the tables.

19. I Thank Marcia Kaplan at the Federal Reserve Bank of New York for providing me with the data.

20. Two other measures were also used: 20-year U.S. Government constant maturity yields; and the difference between the 20-year rate and the preceding day's 3-month T-bill rate. A monthly version of the latter constructed interest rate was also used in Chan, Chen and Hsieh (1985) and Chen, Roll and Ross (1986) to capture the influence of the shape of the term structure. No statistical or economic differences obtained with these estimations, and they are, therefore, not reported in the interest of economy.

21. Because both interest and exchange rates are forward-looking variables (unlike other potential measures of domestic and foreign activity), innovations ought reflect genuine surprises about underlying economic conditions.

22. Sweeney and Warga (1986) find the utilities industry portfolio to be the only portfolio in which an interest rate factor is priced.

23. To check for potential heteroskedasticity in the cross-sectional regression residuals, White's (1980) test was performed. The test proposed in White is to run an OLS regression of the squared estimated residuals from (10) on all second order products and cross-products of the original regressors, or $\eta_i^2 = c + \lambda_i'\alpha + \nu_i$ and test the hypothesis that the α's are jointly zero. No heteroskedasticity was evident in these tests; only the OLS estimates are, therefore, reported in the tables.

24. Alternatively, it may be that the negative sign on the market index reflects the errors-in-variables problem (evidenced by the autocorrelation in EWNY presented in Table 3.1) caused by nonsynchronous daily data. There do exist techniques to take into account the problem of thin trading (Scholes and Williams (1977)). More recently, however, Atchison, Butler and Simonds (1987) find that the autocorrelations present in daily market portfolios returns are not fully explained by thin trading, and that other price-adjustment delay factors need to be examined.

25. Data on industrial production measure its flow during the month, so in order to make this factor contemporaneous with the other factors, changes are led by one month ($IP_t = IP_{t+1}-IP_t$)

26. Unanticipated changes in monthly inflation were also found to be priced by Chen, Roll and Ross (1986), but only over the period 1968-1977.

27. As was the case in Table 3.1, which presents the same statistics for daily observations of the factors, the 3-month Treasury Bill rate is in raw change form, and the exchange rate is specified as the differences of logarithms.

APPENDIX A

THE MONETARY APPROACH TO EXCHANGE RATE DETERMINATION

The standard monetary approach to exchange rate determination is illustrative both of the fundamental variables typically included in equilibrium models and of the central role of the hypothesized expectations formation process.

In the monetary approach the exchange rate is viewed as the relative price of one country's money in terms of another. The money demand equations conventionally used for both the domestic and foreign countries depend on income and interest rates and, for simplicity, many models assume that the elasticities with respect to income and interest rates are identical for both countries:

$$m_t = p_t + \alpha y_t - \beta i_{t,k} \tag{A1}$$

$$m_t^* = p_t^* + \alpha y_t^* - \beta i_{t,k}^* \tag{A2}$$

where, the variables are money (M), prices (P), income (Y), and the exchange rate (S); capital letters denote the level and lower case letters the logarithm; with the exception of the k-period-ahead interest rate ($i_{t,k}$). Foreign variables are denoted with an asterisk *. Goods prices in the two countries are assumed to be perfectly flexible and substitutable so that purchasing power parity holds instantaneously.

$$s_t = p_t - p_t^* \tag{A3}$$

We can solve equations (A1) and (A2) for prices and then substitute in equation (A3) to yield the exchange rate as a function of relative money supplies, income and interest rates.

$$s_t = (m_t - m_t^*) + \alpha(y_t^* - y_t) + \beta(i_{t,k} - i_{t,k}^*) \tag{A4}$$

We can further refine equation (A4) by substituting the covered interest parity condition for the interest differential,

$$i_{t,k} - i^*_{t,k} = f_{t,k} - s_t \tag{A5}$$

where $f_{t,k}$ is the k-period-ahead forward rate. Foreign and domestic bonds are assumed to be perfect substitutes and international arbitrage ensures that speculative efficiency holds, i.e., that the k-period-ahead forward rate equal the k-period-ahead expectation of the spot rate

$$f_{t,k} = E_t s_{t+k} \tag{A6}$$

where E_t represents the mathematical expectation at t. If we combine (A5) and (A6), substitute this in (A4), and let $z_t = (m_t - m^*_t) + \alpha(y^*_t - y_t)$, we arrive at an expression for the exchange rate in terms of relative monies, income and the future exchange rate.

$$s_t = z_t + \beta(E_t s_{t+k} - s_t) \tag{A7}$$

We can now rearrange terms and solve for the reduced form of the exchange rate by process of forward iteration.

$$s_t = \frac{1}{1+\beta}\sum_{k=0}^{\infty}\left[\frac{\beta}{1+\beta}\right]^k E_t z_{t+k} \tag{A8}$$

In the monetarist model, the current spot rate depends on current expectations of all important driving variables (the z's) from now into the indefinite future. The model, while not successful empirically, exemplifies the view that exchange rates are fundamentally dependent on beliefs concerning the future course of monetary policy.

APPENDIX B

EXPECTED AND ACTUAL DM/$ REACTIONS TO FED ANNOUNCEMENTS

Fed policy announcements (1), expected DM/$ spot exchange rate reactions conditional on credibility (2), and actual spot reactions (3) over the period January 1977-February 1981. Score is one if predicted and actual reactions match, denoting a believed announcement. Score is zero if rate moves in opposite direction from that implied by a believed announcement.

Date	Press Abstract of Fed Statement	spot reaction (1)	(2)	(3)
1/24/77	FRB voted slight easing in Fed Funds	–	+	0
3/3/77	Burns warned that Carter's budget deficits could cause an increase in interest rates	+	–	0
4/25/77	FOMC voted for slight easing in monetary policy on March 15	–	–	1
4/29/77	Fed confirms credit tightening	+	–	0
5/11/77	Fed hints at tighter credit reins	+	+	1
5/20/77	Fed gives hint its credit rein might tighten	+	+	1
5/23/77	FOMC voted on May 6 to tighten credit	+	+	1
6/27/77	FOMC voted on May 17 for significant tightening of monetary policy	+	–	0
7/25/77	FOMC voted slight easing of monetary policy at its June 21 meeting	–	+	0
8/2/77	Fed gives hint its target rate is 5 3/4% on federal funds	+	–	0
8/10/77	Fed hints it might be tightening credit	+	–	0
8/12/77	Fed signalled its tightened credit reins	+	+	1
8/15/77	Burns continues drive for tight rein on inflation: in strongest statement yet	+	+	1
8/30/77	FRB increases the discount rate from 5 1/4 to 5 3/4% to bring the rate into better alignment with other short-term rates	+	–	0
9/13/77	Fed confirms tightening credit reins	+	–	0
9/26/77	FOMC voted a tightening of monetary policy	+	+	1

10/3/77	Fed boosts Federal Funds target to 6 3/8%	+	−	0
10/26/77	Fed boosts discount rate from 5 3/4 to 6%	+	+	1
11/2/77	Fed underlined its recent credit tightening allowing Federal Funds rate to rise	+	+	1
11/10/77	Burns strongly defends Fed policy, sets slower money-supply growth	+	−	0
11/21/77	FOMC tightened its monetary policy a notch at its Oct. 18 meeting	+	−	0
12/27/77	FOMC voted for a slight tightening in monetary policy	+	−	0
1/9/78	Fed's decision to boost the discount rate from 6 to 6 1/2% is designed to signal that the U.S. will defend the dollar	+	+	1
1/23/78	FOMC raised the 2-month target growth rates for two key measures of the money supply	−	−	1
1/27/78	Fed underlined its desire to maintain the Federal Funds rate at 6 3/4%	+	+	1
3/6/78	FOMC voted lower goals for money supply	+	−	0
3/10/78	Miller sees possible rise in time-deposit rates	+	+	1
3/27/78	FOMC pared its short-term money supply growth targets at its Feb. 28 meeting	+	−	0
4/5/78	Miller joined the growing ranks of officials who are more pessimistic than Carter about inflation and economic growth	−	−	1
4/21/78	Fed tacitly confirms credit tightening	+	−	0
4/24/78	FOMC voted to expand its target for short term money supply growth on March 21	−	+	0
4/26/78	Miller pledged that the Fed will help fight inflation by 'exercising appropriate restraint' in the conduct of monetary policy	+	−	0
5/11/78	FRB increases the discount rate from 6 1/2 to 7% to bring it into closer alignment with other short−term rates	+	+	1
5/15/78	Miller indicated that the Fed may be able to relax monetary policy before long	−	+	0
5/22/78	Fed gave tacit confirmation that it boosted its federal funds target to 7 1/2 from 7 1/4%	+	−	0

6/8/78	Miller said, Fed doesn't have an agreement with White House to relax its tight monetary policy in exchange for a tougher fiscal policy	+	−	0
6/19/78	Fed seen tightening credit moderately despite worries of a slowing economy	+	−	0
6/23/78	Fed tightened the country's credit spigot another turn	+	−	0
6/27/78	FOMC, at a special meeting temporarily decided against a further tightening of monetary policy	−	+	0
7/3/78	FRB boosted the discount rate from 7 to 7 1/4% to align it with other short rates	+	−	0
7/15/78	FOMC voted to continue to boost the Federal Funds rate to resist inflationary pressures	+	+	1
8/21/78	Fed announced it was raising the discount rate to 7 3/4 from 7 1/4%	+	+	1
8/29/78	Fed tightened nation's credit spigot another turn	+	−	0
9/11/78	In a surprise move, the Fed apparently tightened its credit reins, despite indications that inflation is abating	+	−	0
9/21/78	Fed acts to tighten credit by raising federal funds target rate	+	−	0
9/22/78	FRB raised to discount rate from 7 1/2 to 8%	+	−	0
9/25/78	FOMC voted a tighter credit policy at a special meeting	+	−	0
10/16/78	Discount rate is boosted from 8 to 8 1/2%	+	−	0
10/19/78	Fed worried about persistent inflation and excessive money growth, pulled in its credit reins further	+	−	0
10/23/78	Miller suggested there would be danger in in tightening up too hard and fast on credit in an effort to stem inflation	−	−	1
11/1/78	Carter's anti-inflation (Dollar Defense) package announced--discount rate increased a full percentage from 8 1/2 to 9 1/2%	+	+	1
11/17/78	Miller sees a long fight against inflation with slower growth but no depression	−	−	1

11/24/78	Miller described the duty of monetary-policy makers as 'taking away the punch just when the party is getting good'	+	+	1
11/28/78	FRB may be tightening its credit reins again boosting to 9 7/8% its target interest rate	+	+	1
12/18/78	Miller said Fed may ease monetary rein if 1979 economy heads to deep recession	−	−	1
12/26/78	FOMC keeps tight monetary policy despite slower growth of money supply	+	−	0
1/10/79	Miller said there must be continued austerity in monetary policy to combat inflation, despite the prospect of an economic slowdown	+	+	1
1/19/79	Miller says Fed will continue combating inflation, avoiding recessionary policies	+	+	1
1/26/79	Miller doubts inflation will recede as much as Carter's budget assumes	−	−	1
2/12/79	FOMC voted a tightening of monetary policy at its Dec 19 session	+	+	1
2/15/79	FRB aggressively acts to ease rate rise on federal funds for two days in a row	−	−	1
2/21/79	Fed plan to slow money growth further is signalled in report to Congress	+	+	1
2/23/79	Miller said he doesn't expect inflation to slow 'markedly' this year	−	−	1
3/13/79	Fed gave signs that it hadn't decided to tighten its credit reins as some had expected	−	−	1
4/23/79	A divided FOMC voted to leave monetary policy essentially unchanged but provided for a slight easing if conditions warranted it	−	−	1
5/21/79	FOMC voted to keep credit reins steady despite money-supply gains	−	+	0
6/22/79	Mixed signals prompt an 'even keel' monetary policy but Fed hints it might tighten further	+	−	0
7/18/79	FRB doesn't alter money supply targets though it sees downturn, high inflation	−	−	1
7/20/79	Discount rate increased from 9 1/2 to 10%	+	−	0
8/8/79	Fed zeroed in on a 10 5/8% interest−rate target on federal funds	+	−	0

8/16/79	Fed acts to tighten credit, showing inflation fight persists	+	−	0
8/17/79	Fed raises discount rate to 10 1/2%, a high, in new assault on inflation	+	−	0
8/20/79	FOMC voted a credit tightening July 27	+	−	0
8/24/79	Volcker sees 'monetary discipline' playing a big role in inflation fight	+	−	0
9/6/79	Volcker pledged a continued tight money policy and urged House Budget Committee to hold off loosening fiscal policy through a tax cut	+	−	0
9/19/79	FOMC in a 4−3 vote, tightened credit reins by lifting discount rate to a record 11%	+	−	0
9/24/79	FOMC voted overwhelmingly to tighten credit in August at first two sessions presided over by new chairman, Volcker	+	+	1
10/1/79	Volcker stressed that the U.S. would continue to pursue disciplined budgetary and monetary policies' at a U.S.- W.G. financial meeting	+	−	0
10/6/79	Fed takes strong steps to restrain inflation, shifts monetary tactic (M1 targeting)	+	+	1
10/9/79	Discount rate increased a full percentage point to 12% to assure better control over bank credit	+	+	1
10/19/79	Fed apparently has tightened its credit reins even further	+	+	1
10/29/79	Volcker said that any political pressure on the Fed to ease its policy will be resisted	+	+	1
11/14/79	Volcker says oil price increases could force the Fed to raise its money supply targets for next year	−	−	1
12/13/79	FRB hints at tighter credit policy to reduce loan demand	+	+	1
1/3/80	Volcker declared that any decline in interest rates shouldn't be seen as a sign of easier monetary policy and reemphasized the Fed's determination to maintain the battle against inflation through monetary restraint	+	−	0
2/4/80	Volcker backs Carter's decision not to ask for a tax cut in fiscal 81; cites inflation	+	+	1

2/11/80	FOMC agreed unanimously to reduce slightly its targets for money-supply growth during this year's first quarter	+	−	0
2/15/80	Discount rate increased a full percentage point to 13%	+	+	1
2/20/80	Volcker stressed Fed is determined to cut money-supply growth to fight inflation	+	+	1
3/4/80	Tougher Fed policy hinted, record rise in short-term interest rates in one day	+	+	1
3/14/80	Carter and Fed unveil their long−awaited anti-inflation plans, with credit curb and outlay cut	+	+	1
3/17/80	FRB in new attack on inflation, is stressing restraint on debt rather than higher interest rates	+	+	1
3/19/80	Volcker warned that he would tighten monetary further if current budget-cutting proposals aren't sufficient to dump inflationary pressures	+	+	1
3/24/80	FOMC agreed to let the federal funds rate reach 18%; the increase is consistent with the Fed's new policy of concentrating more on controlling the supply of bank reserves and less on confining short-term fluctuations in the rate itself	+	+	1
4/3/80	Fed eases curb on rise in credit for consumers	−	+	0
4/30/80	FRB further eased its grip on credit costs by allowing a sharp drop in the interest rate on federal funds reserve banks lend to eachother	−	+	0
5/5/80	Fed relaxes money-market credit curbs as pressures mount for an end to tough credit constraints	−	+	0
5/9/80	FRB acted to stem, at least temporarily, the month-long plunge in interest rates; the move surprised many investors	+	+	1
5/15/80	Volcker pledged to stick to current monetary policies despite a slowing economy	+	−	0
5/23/80	FRB eased the credit restraints it imposed in March	−	−	1

5/29/80	FRB lowered to 12% from a record 13% the discount rate	–	+	0
6/13/80	FRB approved a reduction to 11% from 12% in the discount rate it charges on loans to member banks	–	–	1
6/23/80	FRB will take a more cautious approach to easing credit in the weeks ahead; Fed hints 'go-slow' attitude to avoid the risk of rekindling inflationary psychology	+	–	0
7/8/80	FRB as part of a broad move to phase out general credit restraints, decided to end the remaining 7 1/2% reserve requirement on money received by money market funds	–	+	0
7/14/80	FOMC lowered the federal funds rate target to a range of 8 1/2 to 14%	–	+	0
7/25/80	Worried about inflation--Fed toughens stance and decides not to push money growth	+	+	1
7/28/80	Discount rate lowered from 11 to 10% to align it with other short-term rates	–	+	0
7/30/80	FOMC has decided to lower the targets for money growth next year by about 1/2 of a percentage point	+	–	0
8/4/80	Fed vowing to retain 'tight money' policies, prepares for criticism; a collision with Congress, labor and business is feared	+	–	0
8/18/80	FOMC reaffirmed its long-term monetary growth targets and slightly adjusted its short-term targets	+	+	1
9/22/80	FOMC voted to loosen the reins a bit in in the third quarter on nation's money supply	–	+	0
9/26/80	FRB boosted to 11% from 10% the discount rate	+	+	1
10/16/80	A surprise purchase of US T-bills by the Fed sent the interest rate falling in money markets	–	+	0
10/27/80	FOMC voted 8-4 to slow monetary growth and meet 1980 goal	+	+	1
11/17/80	Discount rate increased a full percentage point to 12%	+	–	0
11/24/80	FOMC voted 8-4 to lower the nation's monetary growth targets, making the third tightening in as many months	+	–	0

12/5/80	FRB boosts its discount rate to 13% from 12% rise is second in three weeks	+	+	1
12/23/80	FOMC voted to tighten its credit policy at its NOV 18 meeting and to allow interest rates to rise further	+	–	0
1/8/81	Volcker sees chance to put US economy on the path toward long-term stability	+	+	1
1/28/81	Treasury Secretary Regan and FRB Volcker expressed broad agreement on government action necessary to curb inflation	+	+	1
2/2/81	Fed is expected to continue steady policy as slowing credit demand trims rates	+	–	0
2/6/81	Volcker said there could be a 'perceptible drop' in the inflation rate by year-end if the federal government follows strong anti-inflation policies	+	–	0
2/9/81	FOMC lowered its targets somewhat for growth of money in the first quarter	+	–	0
2/26/81	Volcker said the Fed will follow a restrictive monetary policy that is 'broadly compatible' with the Reagan adminstration's program for cooling inflation	+	+	1

BIBLIOGRAPHY

Adams, Donald and Dale Henderson, "Definition and Measurement of Exchange Market Intervention," Board of Governors of the Federal Reserve System Staff Studies, number 126, 1983.

Akerlof, George A. and Janet Yellen, "Can Small Deviations from Rationality Make Significant Differences to Economic Equilibria?," *American Economic Review*, 1985, 708-735.

Atchison, Michael, Kirt Butler and Richard Simonds, "Nonsynchronous Security Trading and Market Index Autocorrelation," *Journal of Finance*, 1987.

Backus, David and John Driffill, "Inflation and Reputation," *American Economic Review*, 1985, 530-38.

Barro, Robert, "Reputation in a Model of Monetary Policy With Incomplete Information," *Journal of Monetary Economics*, 1986, 3-20.

Barro, Robert and David Gordon, "Rules, Discretion, and Reputation in a Model of Monetary Policy," *Journal of Monetary Economics*, 1983, 101-21.

Bilson, John, "The Speculative Efficiency Hypothesis," *Journal of Business*, 1981, 435-451.

Black, Fischer, Michael Jensen, and Myron Scholes, "The Capital Asset Pricing Model: Some Empirical Results," in *Studies in the Theory of Capital Markets*, edited by Michael Jensen. Praeger, 1972.

Blanchard, Olivier J., "The Lucas Critique and the Volcker Deflation," *American Economic Review*, 1984, 211-215.

Blume, M. E. "Portfolio Theory: A Step Toward Its Practical Application," *Journal of Business*, 1970, 152-73.

Branson, William H., H. Halttunen, and Paul Masson, "Exchange Rates in the Short Run: The Dollar-Deutschemark Rate," *European Economic Review*, 1977, 303-324.

Branson, William, "Exchange Rate Dynamics and Monetary Policy," in *Inflation and Employment in Open Economies*, edited by Assar Lindbeck. North Holland Publishing Company, Amsterdam, 1979.

Brown, R., J. Durbin and J. Evans, "Techniques of Testing for Constancy of Regression Relationships Over Time," *Journal of the Royal Statistic Society* (series B), 1975, 149-163.

Canzoneri, Matthew, "Monetary Policy Games and the Role of Private Information," *American Economic Review*, 1985, 1056-1070.

Carlson, John A. "A Study of Price Forecasts," *Annals of Economic and Social Measurement*, 1977, 27-56.

Chan, K.C., Nai-fu Chen, and David A. Hsieh, "An Exploratory Investigation of the Firm Size Effect," *Journal of Financial Economics*, 1985, 451-471.

Chen, Nai-Fu, Richard Roll, and Stephen A. Ross, "Economic Forces and the Stock Market," *Journal of Business*, 1986, 383-403.

Cho, Chinhyung, Cheol Eun and Lemma Senbet, "International Arbitrage Pricing Theory: An Empirical Investigation," *Journal of Finance*, 1986, 313-329.

Chow, Gregory, "Tests of Equality Between Subsets of Coefficients in Two Linear Regressions," *Econometrica*, 1960, 591-605.

Cornell, Bradford, "Inflation, Relative Price Changes, and Exchange Rate Risk," *Financial Management*, Autumn 1980, 30-34.

Cornell, Bradford, "Money Supply Announcements, Interest Rates and Foreign Exchange," *Journal of International Money and Finance*, 1982, 201-208.

Cukierman, Alex and Allan Meltzer, "A Theory of Ambiguity, Credibility and Inflation Under Discretion and Asymmetric Information," *Econometrica*, 1986, 1099-1128.

Cumby, Robert and Maurice Obstfeld, "A Note on Exchange Rate Expectations and Nominal Interest Differentials: A Test of the Fisher Hypothesis," *Journal of Finance*, 1981, 697-704.

Cumby, Robert and Maurice Obstfeld, "International Interest Rate and Price Level Linkages under Flexible Exchange Rates: A Review of Recent Evidence," in *Exchange Rate Theory and Practice*, edited by Bilson and Marston. University of Chicago Press, 1984, 121-149.

Dhrymes, Phoebus, Irwin Friend and Bulent Gultekin, "A Critical Reexamination of Empirical Evidence on the Arbitrage Pricing Theory," *Journal of Finance*, 1984, 323-346.

Dominguez, Kathryn M., "Are Foreign Exchange Forecasts Rational? New Evidence from Survey Data," *Economics Letters*, 1986, 277-281.

Dominguez, Kathryn M., "Market Responses to Coordinated Central Bank Intervention," *Carnegie-Rochester Series on Public Policy*, 32, 1990a.

Dominguez, Kathryn M., "Have Recent Central Bank Foreign Exchange Intervention Operations Influenced the Yen?," unpublished, 1990b.

Dominguez, Kathryn M., "Foreign Exchange Market Intervention" and "Coordinated Central Bank Intervention," in *The New Palgrave Dictionary of Money and Finance*, edited by J. Eatwell, M. Milgate and P. Newman. Macmillan Press: London, forthcoming 1992.

Dominguez, Kathryn and Jeffrey Frankel, "Does Foreign Exchange Intervention Matter? Disentangling the Portfolio and Expectations Effects," NBER working paper 3299, revised January 1992a.

Dominguez, Kathryn and Jeffrey Frankel, *Intervention Policy Reconsidered*, Policy Analysis in International Economics Series. Institute for International Economics, forthcoming 1992b.

Domowitz, Ian and Craig S. Hakkio, "Conditional Variance and the Risk Premium in the Foreign Exchange Market," *Journal of International Economics*, 1985, 47-66.

Dooley, Michael, "Foreign Exchange Market Intervention," in *The Political Economy of Policy-Making*, edited by Michael Dooley, Herbert Kaufman, and Raymond Lombra. Sage, 1979.

Dooley, Michael and Peter Isard, "A Portfolio-Balance Rational-Expectations Model of the Dollar-Mark Exchange Rate," *Journal of International Economics*, 1982, 257-76.

Dornbusch, Rudiger, "Expectations and Exchange Rate Dynamics," *Journal of Political Economy*, 1976, 1161-76.

Dornbusch, Rudiger, "Flexible Exchange Rates and Interdependence," *IMF Staff Papers*, 1983, 3-30.

Durbin, J. "Tests for Serial Correlation in Regression Analysis Based on the Periodogram of Least Squares Residuals," *Biometrika*, 1969, 1-5.

Edison, Hali, "The Rise and Fall of Sterling: Testing Alternative Models of Exchange Rate Determination," *Applied Economics*, 1985, 1003-21.

Engel, Charles and Jeffrey Frankel, "Why Interest Rates React to Monetary Announcements: An Explanation from the Foreign Exchange Market," *Journal of Monetary Economics*, 1984, 31-39.

Engle, Robert and D.F. Kraft, "Multiperiod Forecast Error Variances of Inflation Estimated from ARCH Models," in *Applied Time Series Analysis of Economic Data*, edited by A. Zellner. Bureau of the Census, 1983.

Fair, Ray C., "Interest Rate and Exchange Rate Determination," Cowles Foundation Discussion Paper, No. 810, 1986.

Fama, Eugene F., "Efficient Capital Markets: A Review of Theory and Empirical Work," *Journal of Finance*, 1970, 383-417.

Fama, Eugene F. and James D. MacBeth, "Risk, Return and Equilibrium: Empirical Tests," *Journal of Political Economy*, 1973, 607-636.

Fama, Eugene F., "Forward and Spot Exchange Rates," *Journal of Monetary Economics*, 1984, 319-338.

Frankel, Jeffrey, "The Diversifiability of Exchange Risk," *Journal of International Economics*, 1982, 379-92.

Frankel, Jeffrey, *Six Possible Meanings of "Overvaluation": The 1981-85 Dollar*, Essays in International Finance, No.159, Princeton University, 1985.

Frankel, Jeffrey and Kenneth Froot, "Using Survey Data to Test Some Standard Propositions Regarding Exchange Rate Expectations," *American Economic Review*, 1987, 133-153.

Frankel, Jeffrey, and Kenneth Froot, "Chartists, Fundamentalists, and the Demand for Dollars," in *Private Behavior and Government Policy in Interdependent Economies*, edited by A. Courakis and M. Taylor. Clarendon Press: Oxford, U.K., 1990a.

Frankel, Jeffrey and Kenneth Froot, "Exchange Rate Forecasting Techniques, Survey Data, and Implications for the Foreign Exchange Market," *American Economic Review* 80, 2, May 1990b, 181-185.

Frenkel, Jacob, "A Monetary Approach to the Exchange Rate: Doctrinal Aspects and Empirical Evidence," *Scandinavian Journal of Economics*, 1976, 200-24.

Frenkel, Jacob, "International Reserves: Pegged Exchange Rates and Managed Float," in *Public Policies in Open Economies*, edited by Brunner and Meltzer. Carnegie-Rochester Conference Series, 1978.

Frenkel, Jacob, "Flexible Exchange Rates, Prices and the Role of 'News': Lessons From the 1970's," *Journal of Political Economy*, 1981, 665-705.

Friedman, Milton, "The Case for Flexible Exchange Rates," in *Essays in Positive Economics*. University of Chicago Press, 1953.

Froot, Kenneth, "Exchange Rate Survey Data: The Role of Expectational Errors, the Risk Premium, and Measurement Error," unpublished, 1985.

Froot, Kenneth, and Jeffrey Frankel, "Forward Discount Bias: Is it an Exchange Risk Premium?," *Quarterly Journal of Economics*, 1989.

Gensberg, Hans, "Effects of Central Bank Intervention in the Foreign Exchange Market," *IMF Staff Papers*, 1981, 451-76.

Gibbons, Michael R., "Multivariate Tests of Financial Models: A New Approach," *Journal of Financial Economics*, 1982, 3-27.

Girton, Lance, and Dale Henderson, "Central Bank Operations in Foreign and Domestic Assets Under Fixed and Flexible Exchange Rates," in *The Effects of Exchange Rate Adjustments* edited by Peter B. Clark, Dennis Logue, and Richard Sweeney. Government Printing Office, 1977.

Green, Margaret, "U.S. Experience with Exchange Market Intervention: September 1977-December 1979," Board of Governors of the Federal Reserve System Staff Studies No. 128, 1984a.

Green, Margaret, "U.S. Experience with Exchange Market Intervention: October 1980- September 1981," Board of Governors of the Federal Reserve System Staff Studies No. 129, 1984b.

Grossman, Jacob, "The 'Rationality' of Money Supply Expectations and Short-Run Response of Interest Rates to Monetary Surprises," *Journal of Money, Credit and Banking*, 1981, 409-424.

Hakkio, Craig, "Expectations and the Forward Exchange Rate," *International Economic Review*, 1981, 663-678.

Hakkio, Craig and Douglas Pearce, "The Reaction of Exchange Rates to Economic News," Federal Reserve Bank of Kansas City Working Paper 8501, 1985.

Haltiwagner, John and Michael Waldman, "Rational Expectations and the Limits of Rationality: An Analysis of Heterogeneity," *American Economic Review*, 1985, 326-340.

Hansen, Lars P.,"Large Sample Properties of Generalized Method of Moments Estimators," *Econometrica*, 1982, 1029-1054.

Hansen, Lars P. and Robert Hodrick, "Forward Rates as Optimal Predictors of Future Spot Rates: An Econometric Analysis," *Journal of Political Economy*, 1980, 829-853.

Hansen, Lars P. and Robert Hodrick, "Risk Averse Speculation in the Forward Foreign Exchange Market: An Econometric Analysis of Linear Models," in *Exchange Rates and International Macroeconomics*, edited by Jacob Frenkel. University of Chicago Press, 1983.

Hardouvelis, Girkas, "Market Perceptions of Federal Reserve Policy and the Weekly Monetary Announcements," *Journal of Monetary Economics*, 1984, 225-240.

Hayashi, Fumio and Christopher Sims, "Nearly Efficient Estimation of Time Series Models with Predetermined But Not Exogenous Instruments," *Econometrica*, 1983, 783-798.

Henderson, Dale, "Exchange Market Intervention Operations: Their Role in Financial Policy and Their effects," in *Exchange Rate Theory and Practice*, edited by Bilson and Marston. NBER Conference Volume, University of Chicago Press, 1984.

Hodrick, Robert J. and Sanjay Srivastava, "An Investigation of Risk and Return in Forward Foreign Exchange," *Journal of International Money and Finance*, 1984, 5-29.

Hooper, Peter and John Morton, "Fluctuations in the Dollar: A Model of Nominal and Real Exchange Rate Determination," *Journal of International Money and Finance*, 1982, 39-56.

Hsieh, David A., "Tests of Rational Expectations and No Risk Premium in Forward Exchange Markets," *Journal of International Economics*, 1984, 173-184.

Huang, R. D., "The Monetary Approach to Exchange Rates in an Efficient Foreign Exchange Market: Tests Bases on Volatility," *Journal of Finance*, 1981, 31-42.

Huizinga, John and Frederic S. Mishkin, "Monetary Policy Regime Shifts and the Unusual Behavior of Real Interest Rates," *Carnegie Rochester Series on Public Policy*, 1986, 231-274.

Ito, Takatoshi, "Foreign Exchange Rate Expectations: Micro Survey Data," *American Economic Review*, 80, 3, 1990, 434-449.

Johnson, Harry, "The Case for Flexible Exchange Rates," *Federal Reserve Bank of St. Louis Review*, 1969, 12-24.

Krasker, W.S., "The 'Peso Problem' in Testing the Efficiency of the Forward Exchange Markets," *Journal of Monetary Economics*, 1980, 269-276.

Kreps, David, and Robert Wilson, "Sequential Equilibria," *Econometrica*, 1982, 863-94.

Kouri, Pentti, and Michael Porter, "International Capital Flows and Portfolio Equilibrium," *Journal of Political Economy*, 1974, 443-67.

Kydland, Finn and Edward Prescott, "Rules Rather Than Discretion: The Inconsistency of Optimal Plans," *Journal of Political Economy*, 1977, 473-93.

Kandel, Shmuel and Robert Stambaugh, "On Correlations and Inferences About Mean-Variance Efficiency," *Journal of Financial Economics*, 1987, 7-27.

Loopesko, Bonnie, "Relationships Among Exchange Rates, Intervention, and Interest Rates: An Empirical Investigation," *Journal of International Money and Finance*, 1984, 257-277.

Mankiw, Gregory N. and Matthew D. Shapiro, "Risk and Return: Consumption Versus Market Beta," *Review of Economics and Statistics*, 1986, 452-59.

McCulloch, John, "Operational Aspects of the Siegal Paradox," *Quarterly Journal of Economics*, 1975, 170-175.

Mishkin, Frederic S., "Are Market Forecasts Rational?," *American Economic Review*, June 1981, 295-306.

Meese, Richard A. and Kenneth Rogoff, "Empirical Exchange Rate Models of the Seventies: Do They Fit Out-of-Sample?," *Journal of International Economics*, 1983, 3-24.

Meese, Richard A. and Kenneth Rogoff, "Was It Real? The Exchange Rate-Interest Differential Relation, 1973-1984," Federal Reserve Board International Finance Discussion Paper, No.268, 1985.

Meese, Richard A. and Kenneth J. Singleton, "On Unit Roots and the Empirical Modeling of Exchange Rates," *Journal of Finance*, 1982, 1029-1035.

Mussa, Michael, "The Exchange Rate, the Balance of Payments, and Monetary Policy Under a Regime of Controlled Floating," *Scandinavian Journal of Economics*, 1976, 229-48.

Mussa, Michael, "The Role of Official Intervention," *Group of Thirty Occasional Papers*, New York: Group of Thirty, 1981.

Mussa, Michael, "A Model of Exchange Rate Dynamics," *Journal of Political Economy*, 1982, 74-103.

Muth, John F., "Rational Expectations and the Theory of Price Movements," *Econometrica*, 1961, 315-335.

Nordhaus, William D. and Steven Durlauf, "Empirical Tests of the Rationality of Economic Forecasters: A Fixed Horizon Approach," Cowles Foundation Discussion Paper No. 717r, 1984, 1-40.

Obstfeld, Maurice, "Imperfect Asset Substitutability and Monetary Policy Under Fixed exchange Rates," *Journal of International Economics*, 1980, 177-200.

Obstfeld, Maurice, "Exchange Rates, Inflation, and the Sterilization Problem: Germany, 1975-1981," *European Economic Review*, 1983, 161-89.

Obstfeld, Maurice, "The Effectiveness of Foreign-Exchange Intervention: Recent Experience: 1985-1988," in *International Policy Coordination and Exchange Rate Fluctuations*, edited by Branson, Frenkel, and Goldstein. NBER Conference Volume, University of Chicago Press, Chicago, 1990.

Rogoff, Kenneth, "Time-series Studies of the Relationship Between Exchange Rates and Intervention: A Review of the Techniques and the Literature," Board of Governors of the Federal Reserve System Staff Studies, No. 132, 1983.

Rogoff, Kenneth, "On the Effects of Sterilized Intervention. An Analysis of Weekly Data," *Journal of Monetary Economics*, 1984, 133-150.

Roll, Richard, "A Critique of the Asset Pricing Theory's Tests, Part I: On Past and Potential Testability of the Theory," *Journal of Financial Economics*, 1977, 129-176.

Ross, Stephen A., "The Arbitrage Theory of Capital Asset Pricing," *Journal of Economic Theory*, 1976, 341-360.

Ross, Stephen A., "The Determination of Financial Structure: The Incentive Signalling Approach," *Bell Journal of Economics*, 1977, 23-39.

Scholes, Myron and J. Williams, "Estimating Betas from Nonsynchronous Data," *Journal of Financial Economics*, 1977, 309-360.

Shanken, Jay, "Multivariate Proxies and Asset Pricing Relations: Living With the Roll Critique," *Journal of Financial Economics*, 1987, 91-110.

Shiller, Robert, John Campbell, and Kermit Schoenholtz, "Forward Rates and Future Policy: Interpreting the Term Structure of Interest Rates," *Brookings Papers on Economic Activity*, 1983, 173-223.

Siegel, Jeremy J., "Risk, Interest, and Forward Exchange," *Quarterly Journal of Economics*, 1972, 303-9.

Solnik, Bruno, "International Parity Conditions and Exchange Rate Risk," *Journal of Banking and Finance*, 1978, 281-293.

Solnik, Bruno, "International Arbitrage Pricing Theory," *Journal of Finance*, 1983, 449-457.

Stambaugh, Robert F., "On the Exclusion of Assets from Tests of the Two-Parameter Model: A Sensitivity Analysis," *Journal of Financial Economics*, 1982, 237-268.

Stockman, Alan, "Monetary Control and Sterilization Under Pegged exchange Rates," University of Rochester, unpublished, 1979.

Stockman, Alan, "A Theory of Exchange Rate Determination," *Journal of Political Economy*, 88, August 1980, 673-695.

Struth, Friedrich K., "Modelling Expectations Formation with Parameter-Adaptive Filters: An Empirical Application to the Livingston Forecasts," *Oxford Bulletin of Economics and Statistics*, 1984, 211-239.

Sweeney, Richard J. and Arthur D. Warga, "The Pricing of Interest-Rate Risk: Evidence From the Stock Market," *Journal of Finance*, 1986, 393-410.

Tobin, James, "A General Equilibrium Approach to Monetary Theory," *Journal of Money, Credit, and Banking*, 1969, 15-29.

Tryon, Ralph, "Testing for Rational Expectations in Foreign Exchange Markets," Federal Reserve Board International Finance Discussion Paper, No. 139, 1979.

Urich, Thomas and Paul Wachtel, "The Informational Content of Weekly Money Supply Announcements in the 1970s," *Journal of Finance*, 1981, 1063-1072.

Watson, Mark, "Applications of Kalman Filter Models in Econometrics," Ph.D. Dissertation, 1980, UCSD.

Watson, Mark and Robert Engle, "Testing for Regression Coefficient Stability with a Stationary AR(1) Alternative," *The Review of Economics and Statistics*, 1985, 341-346.

White, Halbert, "A Heteroskedasticity-Consistent Covariance Matrix Estimator and a Direct Test for Heteroskedasticity," *Econometrica*, 1980, 817-838.

Williamson, John, *The Exchange Rate System*, Policy Analysis in International Economics, No. 5, Institute for International Economics, 1983.

Wonnacott, Paul, "US Intervention in the Exchange Market for DM, 1977-80," Princeton Studies in International Finance, 51, 1982.

Zellner, Arnold, "An Efficient Method of Estimating Seemingly Unrelated Regressions and Tests of Aggregation Bias," *Journal of the American Statistical Association*, 57, 1962, 348-368.

INDEX

For Product Safety Concerns and Information please contact our EU representative GPSR@taylorandfrancis.com Taylor & Francis Verlag GmbH, Kaufingerstraße 24, 80331 München, Germany

Batch number: 10725973

Printed by Printforce, the Netherlands